HISTORY OF THE
14TH GEORGIA
INFANTRY REGIMENT

Ray Dewberry

HERITAGE BOOKS
2008

HERITAGE BOOKS
AN IMPRINT OF HERITAGE BOOKS, INC.

Books, CDs, and more—Worldwide

For our listing of thousands of titles see our website
at
www.HeritageBooks.com

Published 2008 by
HERITAGE BOOKS, INC.
Publishing Division
100 Railroad Ave. #104
Westminster, Maryland 21157

International Standard Book Number: 978-1-58549-913-7

MAPS

ACKNOWLEDGEMENT

I am extremely grateful and completely indebted to my uncle Sidney Oliver Dewberry who suggested this work. Throughout he has provided encouragement with multiple telephone conversations and has provided financial backing in the form of allowing me to use the clerical staff and illustrators of his business firm to edit the text and to make many of the maps that appear in this text. He has provided his own reviews of the text and suggested many changes as well as arranged for an external professional review. He also made the initial contact with this publisher. Without his help this book would not have been started, completed, or published. His first cousin Sidney Alton Dewberry conducted much of the original research and made it available to me as a starting point. Private Aaron Jackson Dewberry of the 14th GA infantry was their grandfather as well as my great-grandfather. Sidney Alton also provided continuous encouragement to get this work completed and spent a day with me in Barnwell SC getting much of the text in its near final form. Catherine Bohn performed the illustration and graphics for several of the maps in this book. Debbi Ishmael edited and formatted the text.

HISTORY OF THE 14TH GEORGIA INFANTRY REGIMENT

INTRODUCTION

This is an accounting of the movements and combat history of the 14th Georgia Infantry regiment of the Confederate States Army, in which our ancestor Aaron Jackson Dewberry served from March 1862 until April 1865. Much of this history was derived from letters written by 14th Georgia veterans that offer an eyewitness journal of the regiment's experiences. From the many references to Company A, to members therein, and to Monroe County Georgia, it is clear the bulk of the material was written by one or more members in Company A, the very company in which Aaron Jackson and his brother James served.

In this report, we have attempted to weave an historical perspective into the personal accounting. Much of the report consists of quotations from eyewitnesses. Clearly, they tell the story best. We have added a narrative that we believe helps tell the story. We hope the descendants of Aaron Jackson will read this with pride in the personal sacrifices he and his fellow soldiers made.

We write this with great pride in our ancestor. We do not write to glorify the time or the war in which he participated. Many 20th century Americans are inclined to do so. But let us remember that this was a long and very bloody war. The men of both armies fought and died for their countries in the truest sense of the phrase. Those of us who tend to dream of the glory of the Confederate Army, an almost incomparable army, must remember that the enemy (from the perspective of the 14th) was the United States Army, the same army as that of George Washington, John Pershing, Dwight Eisenhower, and of many of AJ's descendants. This army shed the greater amount of blood to preserve what the Confederate Army was attempting to destroy.

Still, we can honor the Confederate veterans of this regiment. The personal sacrifices they made, the personal misery they endured, and the losses in killed and wounded they sustained are a testament to the hardy and courageous souls they possessed. In the chapter entitled "The Landing at Kuralie" in his book Tales of the South Pacific, James Michener gives an excellent perspective on what small portion of men at war actually fight the enemy. Even of those actually at the scene of battle, only a few really trade rounds with the enemy. Only a few know what war is; the rest of us will never know. The men of the 14th Georgia, the 119 men of Company A, fought the enemy. For seven desperate days near Richmond in 1862; for a day at Cedar Mountain and a day at 2nd Manassas; for a day of bloody victory at Fredericksburg; for two days of offensive gambling at Chancellorsville; for three days of tragedy at Gettysburg; for a spring and summer of attrition in the Virginia Wilderness; and at a final stand at Petersburg, the 14th Georgia fought the enemy.

Thanks to the surviving records of that era, we have a detailed accounting of the losses sustained throughout the four-year period. We have an exact knowledge by name and rank of the 1194 men of this regiment. Of Aaron Jackson's Company A, only two men are not accounted for. Over the war Company A suffered 55 casualties in dead and wounded. With other losses from illness and discharge, only 27 men remained to surrender at Appomattox Courthouse on 9 April 1865.

Finally, before we begin our story, we place the regiment in Lee's Army. The 14th started the war in Wade Hampton's brigade of General Joseph E. Johnston's army. Lee did not obtain command until the Peninsula Campaign of 1862. By the Seven Days battle near Richmond in June 1862 the 14th was part of a Georgia brigade in A. P. Hill's division. After the Seven Days, Hill's division joined Jackson's Corps for the battles of 2nd Manassas, Antietam Creek, Fredericksburg, and Chancellorsville. With Jackson's death at Chancellorsville, A. P. Hill became corps commander, and Brigadier General Pender attained command of the division. When Pender was killed at Gettysburg, Major General Wilcox of Longstreet's Corps became division commander. For most of the war Brigadier General E. L. Thomas commanded the Georgia brigade that contained the 14th GA. Regimental and company commanders changed frequently, and we will follow those changes in our story.

ANTEBELLUM YEARS

Aaron Jackson Dewberry was born and raised in Monroe County, Georgia. Located in central Georgia just north of the city of Macon, Monroe County came into existence only twenty-four years prior to "Jack" Dewberry's birth in 1845. Monroe, like the rest of the "black belt" region of antebellum central Georgia, had an agricultural economy based on the production of cotton on large plantations. In 1860, Monroe's residents raised 17,165 bales of cotton weighing approximately 400 pounds each. The county's other main crops included Indian corn, wheat, sweet potatoes, peas, and beans.

The 1860 United States Census lists the names of 5,753 white people and the age and sex of 10,177 African-American slaves who resided in Monroe County. At least a half dozen white families in Monroe were named Dewberry, all undoubtedly related in one way or another. The heads of all but one Dewberry household appear on the census as farmers, several having acquired the coveted status of planter. Sixty-four-year-old Thomas F. Dewberry was the wealthiest of the lot, owning $125,000 in real and personal estate, including fifty-three slaves.

Jack Dewberry's father, James William Dewberry Sr. was clearly one of the least prosperous of the Monroe County Dewberrys in 1860 in terms of his wealth in real and personal estate. James Sr. appears as a farmer in the 1850 census, but in 1860 he is listed as the Monroe County jailer, living with his family in the county seat of Forsyth. According to family traditions, James Dewberry Sr.'s family supplemented their household income by producing and selling chairs and straw hats made in part from strips of white oak tree bark.

Along with fifty-five-year-old James William Sr. and Aaron Jackson (listed simply as "Jack" on the 1850 and 1860 Census), the Dewberry household included four other members in 1860. Fifty-year-old Julian A. Landrum Dewberry was James Sr.'s wife. James Sr.'s and Julian's three additional children included Elizabeth Julian, a twenty-two-year-old milliner; seventeen-year-old Rhoda Clemenia, who had been a student in 1850; and twenty-year-old James William Dewberry Jr. James Jr. appears as a mechanic on the 1860 census, and undoubtedly spent much of his time repairing cotton gins and other types of farm machinery in one of several workshops in Forsyth.

Although James Sr. owned a house lot in Forsyth and had contracted to build a house on it on February 18, 1859, the family apparently had not finished the building or moved into it when the census taker visited them in 1860. The 1860 census indicates that they lived in quarters attached to or immediately adjacent to the wooden county jail located at the corner of West Chambers and South Phelps Streets on the southwest corner of the courthouse square in Forsyth.

The Dewberrys found their lives changed forever in the winter of 1860-1861, when the election of Abraham Lincoln as U.S. President prompted the secession of several Southern states. Within weeks after Georgia's secession from the Union in late January 1861, dozens of eager young men in Monroe County organized a military company known as the "Quitman Guards." In late March 1861, the Guards left Monroe amidst great fanfare to join the First Georgia Volunteers, organized in Macon on April 3, 1861.

3

John Hunter Etheridge, a twenty-eight-year-old physician living and practicing in Forsyth, organized the second military company in Monroe County, the "Confederate Volunteers." Etheridge, a member of the University of Georgia class of 1854, was "a man of fine personal appearance, engaging manners, and of high standing socially and professionally." When the "Confederate Volunteers" mustered into the Confederate Army for the duration of the war on July 9, 1861, the popular Captain Etheridge had 86 volunteers. (A total of 119 men served in the "Confederate Volunteers" during the Civil War.) Most of these men lived in Forsyth or were farmers, overseers, and day laborers from the surrounding districts. James William Dewberry Jr., a Forsyth neighbor of Etheridge, was one of the Confederate Volunteers, as was James Jr's second cousin, Berry W. Dewberry. (Berry W. Dewberry apparently survived the Civil War, spending much of his Confederate Army service in hospitals in Virginia and Georgia. His various travels in and out of these hospitals are not covered in this essay.)

FIRST BLOOD

When Lincoln called for volunteers in April 1861 to stop the rebellion in the South, thousands quickly volunteered on both sides to participate in what both sides anticipated would be a short war. While Northern forces clearly had the long-term advantage of a larger population and greater industrial might, many historians believe the Southern forces had the short-term advantage of better military preparedness. Of course no regular Confederate Army forces existed, but in 1861 U.S. regular Army forces totaled only 16,000. From these, many officers resigned to join the Confederacy. The US lost most of its best combat leaders to the Confederacy including Braxton Bragg, P.G.T. Beauregard, Joseph Johnston, Albert Sidney Johnston, A.P. Hill, R.E. Lee, and J.E.B. Stuart. Thomas Jackson and D.H. Hill were teaching at Southern military schools and joined the Confederate Army to quickly become dominant factors in the war.

The bulk of both armies were formed in the traditional way. Volunteer regiments were raised and equipped by the individual states. Captains and lieutenants were elected by the troops, and colonels, lt. colonels, and majors were appointed by state governors and legislatures. The 14th was officially formed on 9 July 1861 and was quickly rushed to Virginia for arming and training. Aaron Jackson's older brother James volunteered in this group and went north with it in Monroe County's Company A. By late July the regiment was in Northern Virginia, but did not participate in the first Manassas battle on 21 July. The 14th GA infantry regiment was organized at first as follows:

Company Letter	Company Names	Commander	County
A	Confederate Volunteers	John H. Etheridge	Monroe
B	Ramah Guards	Robert Folsom	Wilkinson
C	Jasper Light Infantry	Charles Jordan	Jasper
D	Cherokee Brown Rangers	James Fielder	Cherokee
E	Lester Volunteers	Richard Lester	Forsyth
F	Johnson Greys	Robert Harmon	Johnson
G	Yancey Independents	William Harris	Worth
H	Blackshear Guards	Thomas Yopp	Laurens
I	Jeff Davis Rifles	Rufus McMichael	Butts
J	Etowah Guards	Thomas Jones	Bartow

At 1st Manassas, Generals Joseph Johnston and P.G.T. Beauregard defeated McDowell's US force, sending them running out of Virginia. This tactical defeat for the North might have been a strategic victory. It served to give the US forces a wake-up call, while fueling the popular Confederate notion that one Southerner could whip six Yankees. After the battle, Major General McClellan was appointed to command and to train US forces. His initiative and self-inflating personality were later found wanting by Lincoln, but historians agree he trained the Northern forces well, and he further proved a good tactical leader in combat. Very little fighting occurred in Virginia for the next ten months. Johnston's army manned the south bank of the Potomac, and McClellan's trained in and around Washington.

After 1st Manassas, the 14th's first assignment directed them to western Virginia where they served briefly under a former Virginia governor, General John B. Floyd. For most of the rest of 1861 the 14th was in western Virginia where many suffered from the unexpected cold. Four of Co. A died of disease. On November 4, the 14th was transferred to the command of Wade Hampton's brigade of Joseph Johnston's army on the Potomac. On December 9, Colonel Brumley resigned, and also on that date many troops of the 14th were discharged as disabled or undesirable. Felix Price was promoted to Lt. Colonel and was given command of the regiment.

The 14th Georgia's first campaign was "remarkable in the history of the regiment for the sickness and suffering" the men endured. Privates James and Berry Dewberry and their comrades were "raw men, ignorant of camp life, unused to exposures of wet and cold, and the fatigues of marching." Measles and mumps broke out and spread through the 14th. While fighting these diseases, many men contracted colds and fevers. "The medical department was unorganized," remembered one Georgian, "the supply of medicine wholly inadequate, and the accommodations for the sick of the very poorest kind." At one point while in western Virginia, only 120 men in the 14th reported for duty out of the 770 who had left Lynchburg in late July 1861. Deaths and discharges due to disease ravaged the entire regiment, including Captain Etheridge's company.

In late winter 1862, Lieutenant Jordan obtained 15 recruits for his company, enrolling them into the Confederate Army on March 4, 1862, in Forsyth, probably during the mustering of the Monroe County militia. Aaron Jackson Dewberry was one of Jordan's 15 recruits that received the $50 bounty for enlisting for the term of three years or the duration of the war. Jack Dewberry probably enlisted in the "Confederate Volunteers" for both patriotic and personal reasons. Like most young men, he undoubtedly desired to avoid the stigma of being drafted and labeled a conscript. Enlisting in the "Confederate Volunteers" also allowed him to serve alongside many men he had known his entire life, including his brother and cousin.

In March, Aaron Jackson and 15 other new privates joined Co. A near Fredericksburg. In this whole group, the regiment added over 100 soldiers, bringing its strength to about 1,000. In mid-April, Hampton's brigade was ordered south to the York and James River Peninsula in anticipation of McClellan's spring campaign to take Richmond from the east. The brigade was temporarily assigned to Whiting's division.

In the spring campaign, McClellan's original plan called for an attack on the peninsula formed by the York and Rappahanock Rivers. Lee (on staff duty in Richmond) and Davis anticipated that possibility and assigned Major General Magruder's division to that northern peninsula. Here Magruder's division of about 20,000 performed the first of two brilliant acting jobs, convincing McClellan the York-Rappahanock peninsula was manned by a huge army. McClellan switched his attack to the York-James peninsula, which Lee and Davis preferred and which Lincoln did not. Hampton's brigade waited there along with the bulk of Johnston's army.

In late April and early May, Johnston's outnumbered army manned the defensive trenches near Yorktown. McClellan poured in his huge army, but refused to attack head-on with his infantry. The 14th GA experienced its first mortar attack on the evening of May 1. Shortly, the Confederate Army stealthily pulled out leaving Yorktown and most of the peninsula to US forces. Aaron Jackson and the 14th saw their first action on May 6 with a successful bayonet charge at New Kent courthouse. US resistance was poor, and the 14th suffered no casualties while taking several prisoners. With a company strength of 90, the war had started in earnest for this group of Monroe County fighters. From the letters sent home by the young Company A soldiers, we gain the beginning accounts. The quotations below begin on July 9, 1861, and take us to mid-May 1862.

"We were ordered to meet at the Forsyth Courthouse on July 9th. It was a short meeting with most of the time devoted to defining honor and duty. The short of it was giving all members one week to take care of personal business and meet at the train depot for departure on July 15th morning. Although James Jordan was very instrumental in organizing Company A, he was not elected its captain. Instead, this honor went to Dr. John H. Etheridge, Bill Haupt as first lieutenant, and Jeff Hogan as first sergeant. There were also additional lieutenants, sergeants, as well as corporals elected. On July 15, 1861, nothing went right. The train was on time but the young men were not and also a goodly fourth were carrying three times the amount of personal effects allowed. So, what to keep and what to send back home seemed to baffle the most brilliant among us and this to the complete anguish of Doctor Etheridge and the train conductor. Finally, with five missing and seventy-two safely aboard, the train left with tempers flaring. Nor did such decrease as the morning progressed because of the constant stops at every pig path between Forsyth and Atlanta picking up small groups along the way. A trip, which otherwise should have been two hours, ends up being four. Before reaching the large city, we disembarked and walked two miles into an area called Cabbagetown community and into a large schoolyard. The old school was in bad disrepair and everywhere therein a human body occupied space. Tents occupied the surrounding outer regions with the middle reserved for training. For every real rifle, there were fifty with long sticks marching to and fro and mostly out of step. So it went for two days. July 17th we met on the side of the schoolhouse with some sharply dressed Confederate staff officers conducting. We were organized into a regiment which consisted of ten companies. 14th commanding officers were Colonel Arnoldus Brumby, Lieutenant Colonel Whiteford Ramsey, and Major Felix Price. Additionally, we raised our right arm to the square and swore allegiance and life to our officers and to the Confederate States of America. Around noon we formed and marched to the railroad and departed with a half-strength regiment of eight hundred men and almost no guns. By Georgia rail we went first to Branchville, South Carolina. The Mexican War veterans among us were having a field day; say they, "When the Yankees see this crowd, they will laugh themselves to death and victory is ours."

"Changing trains at Branchville, we boarded the South Carolina Railroad to Columbia, South Carolina, disembarked, and camped overnight in an open field near the railroad junction. We observed thousands of Florida men headed north by rail. The North Carolina Railroad rook over and the following morning we were on our way to Danville, Virginia. Again we changed trains to the Richmond-Danville Railroad and went to Burkville, Virginia: again a change to the Virginia-Tennessee Railroad and on to Lynchburg, Virginia arriving there on July 21st, a Sunday morning. The final train change was to the Orange and Alexandria Railroad; however, we remained in Lynchburg for a week's training by a company of Mexican War veterans well trained in the art of battle. It was at this place leaving Lynchburg that every man was armed with his own rifle. Leaving Lynchburg on July 29th, we arrived in Staunton, Virginia. It was here that we learned of the big battle of Manassas on the 21st and where the Yankees had received a well deserved tail kicking. This news put everyone in high spirits. Leaving Staunton, Virginia by foot, we marched over one hundred miles to Huntersville, Virginia in zigzag fashion to confuse the enemy, if they were watching. The weather was terrible. The food was fresh but cooked horribly. The countryside was beautiful. We moved into an area northwest of Huntersville in an open field and here we remained for a week ever in training. Afterward, the army, with us as part, moved up near Cheat Mountain with the obvious intent to again challenge the Federal army stationed there. But as the calendar moved into September, and the attack date neared, the weather had not been taken into sufficient account. Although Virginia soldiers appeared to be at home with the elements, not so with the deep south newcomers. A few days ago, we were in 90-degree heat, now the days are cool and nights downright freezing. Few possessed adequate clothing for the moist night air. The marches and guard duty around the clock were exhaustive. Missing home was demoralizing. A combination of all of these conditions devastated the ranks by creating an epidemic of mumps, measles, flu, common colds, plus many diseases, which doctors could not identify. A full fourth of our regiment were hospitalized. By September 2nd, four were dead and multitudes not expected to live. Attack plans for Cheat Mountain were postponed and on September 6th were canceled until further notice. By September 10th, the death toll was up to ten with some recovery. Many wagons arrived to transport the most sickly to Rockbridge Alum Springs. On September 12th and 13th, we could hear cannon assaulting Cheat Mountain but we participated not and continued caring for the sick among us. Rains were a daily occurrence. We broke camp and returned to Valley Mountain on September 23rd and went into temporary camp. On the 27th, we marched toward Greenbridge. Heard fighting in the direction Greenbriar and changed direction and marched toward Elray and prepared for winter quarters. Here we made extensive plans for staying the winter such as building log cabins, caves, and huts. On October 12th we relocated to another camp on New River which was claimed to be more defendable Col. Brumley in a meeting stated he was leaving for Richmond to protest our location and conditions and wanted his regiment out of the area; if not, he would resign. He took all personal things with him. On October 20, 1861, we are still camped on New River, Western Virginia, a place some of the natives call Martins Bottom. Some previously sick returned by wagon from Rockbridge Alum Springs but still others were placed aboard the same wagons and sent away to the same Hospital. Major Felix Price assumed command of the 14th. We remained in our present location until November 1st whereon we broke camp and marched back to Staunton, Virginia. More training from the Mexico Old Soldier's group until November 14th at which time Major Felix Price called the 14th together and read special order number 222 ordering the 14th Georgia and the 16th North Carolina to march to Mount Jackson and by way of Strasburg go by rail to Manassas and thereat be placed under the command of General J.E. Johnston. Everybody was wild with joy. At first we had thought we were heading back into the mountains after a brief rest period at Staunton. By the 21st of November we were disembarking at Manassas Junction, a real large train junction. Again Major Price called the 14th together to announce the resignation of Colonel Brumley. On November 26th, we as a regiment were assigned to General Wade Hampton's brigade. We immediately marched over to the Bacon Race Churchyard at Dumfries, Virginia and joined the rest of the brigade at that location. After arriving, the temporary regimental commander Major Felix Price officially replaced Colonel Brumley.

On December 20, 1861, we marched over to Colchester, Virginia to assist in the construction of fortifications along the mouth of the Occoquan River. The routine was one day cementing logs into breastworks and the next to picket duty on Wolf Run Shoal. From General Beauregard's Headquarters comes written news of ten privates per company that will be allowed to go home for Christmas, with a limit of 100 from each regiment. Lots will be drawn and winners may designate another if he so desires. A toe sack of Virginia tobacco leaves or two gallons of mountain dew rum could usually influence some winner.

Hampton's brigade this 8th day of January 1862, consists of Hampton's Legions, 16th North Carolina, 14th Georgia, and 19th Georgia regiments and we moved yesterday over to Davis' Ford on the Occoquan Creek. Eight members of each company of the 14th is being sent back to his home county to help entice enlistments to this outfit. Such leave would not count from regular furlough time. Those selected caused much ill-will in camp. First sergeant was accused of playing favorites by sending home snitches who tell him things. Complainers got no rations that evening and extra duty for two days. Lt. Jim Jordan in charge with Sgt. Baldy Davis and other recruiters left for Forsyth, Georgia, February 8th.

Camp life consists during winter months of endless training such as playing ball, writing letters, and reading the bible during rainy and or snowy days. Foraging for food was a daily chore such as rabbit hunting. Most deer were gone with such heavy concentration of militia in the area. Farmers were terrified at these overnight military camps as chickens and livestock would disappear with great rapidity and the who, what, and where of it would vanish come dawn. On March 7th, 1862, we moved from Davis' Ford to Camp Bartow located near the City of Fredericksburg, Virginia. Our brigade now consists of the 14th Georgia, 16th North Carolina, Hampton's Legion, and Moody's Battery of Artillery from Louisiana State.

On April 15, 1862, we are ordered to proceed to the Yorktown-Warwick battle line under General Whiting's Division. The following day on April 16th, we were treated to another shock. The so-called "twelve month enlistment" has now turned into "duration of the war enlistment"; so states the law passed by the Confederate congress and President Jefferson Davis. This caused much anguish not heretofore known in camp because everyone was talking in terms of being home in just two more months. To date, the 14th Georgia had fought no battle nor experienced even a skirmish and void of anyone going AWOL, and certainly no desertions. But in two days time from the enlistment extensions, that is April 19th, two men had walked off from this company with similar happenings throughout. And to hear complaints as one moved around the camp, half were going to do likewise. The

Louisiana outfit caught one of theirs below Richmond walking home, or at least the provost guard did, and returned him by wagon on the 21st morning and was shot that afternoon at 2 PM with the roll of five drums. This had a chilling effect on walk offs and for that matter even talking about it. What had heretofore appeared as minor is placed now in the most serious light.

On the 25th of April, 1862, we marched away from camp Bartow and headed south to Richmond to work on that city's fortifications and so that went until April 28th, whereupon the entire brigade marched within sight of Williamsburg. Nothing much happened here until the evening of the 1st of May 1862, when mortar rounds began to explode in a minor way at first but increased as the day wore on and stopped at nightfall. We are in well constructed ditches with breastworks at one hundred yard intervals. But this helped little the following morning when cannon exploded all over the area and so it went for most of the day. We kept hearing rumors that other outfit had attacked Federal fortifications without success. Whiting's army pulled out of the whole area. Our brigade was last out, being the rear guard. Nor was it a real problem pull out, for the Yankees fully expected us to attack their army and while they waited we simply left without opposition. Since scattered shells continued to pound our now left behind fortifications, we supposed they feel we are still there. We marched on the main turnpike toward James City County Courthouse and camped near Blevin's Mill near Barhamsville until the morning of the 5th of May 1862. A detachment of Jubal Early's cavalry rode in and a conference which lasted two hours took place. After their departure we trained two hours at bayonet practice with several cuttings among us. We broke camp at 1 PM and continued up the pike at an unusual hard pace of march and went an hour past Slaterville, Virginia, and again into camp. More bayonet practice continued and more picket duty that night. Rumors abound of a Yankee force ahead of us blocking our path to Richmond. At 3 AM we made ready for battle and moved slowly up the pike leaving behind guards over our wagons and personal bags. We deployed a mile from New Kent Courthouse and at dawn on May 6th we charged triple time toward enemy lines with bayonets in place and overran their lines, sweeping even past the courthouse in five minutes time with many Yankees captured. Our regiment had fourteen prisoners and most of them taken from closets and attic of the courthouse. Despite complaints from some local citizens, by 11AM we marched toward Richmond with our prisoners and their equipment. But around half past four complaints became intense about exhaustion. Up half the night and pressures of the morning battle had taken its toll and the stop and encampment was granted on the York River near Saint James Church. Most all, except pickets, were asleep before nightfall and apparently some of them as two prisoners got away during the night. On Wednesday, May 7th, 1862, we resumed our march to Richmond and delivered the enlisted ranks of Yankee prisoners to the provost and their officers to a nearby Richmond warehouse and thereafter rejoined our brigade on the east side digging trenches and positioning eight-foot stakes outside breastworks. Preparations are extensive with dirt flying for miles as we fully expect Yankee activity in this area in about a week."

FAIR OAKS

During the spring of 1862, the Confederate Army faced 90,000 troops of McClellan on the peninsula and about 40,000 troops under Banks and McDowell in the northern Shenandoah Valley. Lee and Davis regarded McClellan as the main threat to Richmond, but kept Jackson in the Valley with the sole purpose of preventing Banks and McDowell from joining McClellan against Johnston. This reasoning worked masterfully. McClellan repeatedly requested that McDowell's Corps join him on the peninsula, but Lincoln kept McDowell and Banks north specifically to defend Washington against Jackson.

The Confederate plan called for a swift combined stroke from Jackson and Joseph Johnston to defeat McClellan near Richmond. Quick movement by Jackson would be required to prevent US forces in the Shenandoah from joining the action.

As McClellan advanced up the James River-York River peninsula, the Chickahominy River became an important feature of the coming battles. Flowing from north of Richmond southeast, it joins the James about midway between Richmond and Hampton. Normally a shallow river, the heavy May rains had made the Chickahominy a raging torrent in the spring of 1862. McClellan advanced on the northern side of the river and on May 31 had only two corps (about 40,000 troops) on the southern side, facing Richmond from the east. With his entire army south of the Chickahominy, Johnston struck McClellan's two corps on May 31 near Fair Oaks, seven miles east of the capitol. Here was fought the two-day battle of Fair Oaks (Seven Pines). Aaron Jackson's 14th GA saw extensive and bloody action.

Late in May the Hampton brigade had been reorganized from Whiting's division into Major General A. P. Hill's division. With A. P. Hill, the brigade would gain many battle stars and streamers, and the men would evolve into experienced combat veterans. Hampton's brigade had operated throughout the spring north of the Chickahominy. On May 28, it crossed to the southern side, joining the bulk of Johnston's army. Johnston's attack on 31 May included AJ's 14th GA and all of Hampton's brigade.

Company A of the 14th GA entered the fighting at Fair Oaks with 88 combatants. Brigadier General Wade Hampton commanded the brigade, Colonel Felix Price had the regiment, and Captain John Etheridge had the company. The Confederate attacks were badly mismanaged. Many divisions were unable to locate their prescribed attack positions. All divisions, and often even brigades, attacked piecemeal instead of together as Johnston intended. The attack nevertheless drove the US left (southern flank) back a mile through the village of Seven Pines. On the US extreme right, a division of Lt. General Sumner's Corps got across the Chickahominy using swaying bridges that were themselves several inches under water, and halted the Confederate advance. The next day, US forces regained all of the ground lost to the Confederates.

During the battle Company A's Captain Etheridge was killed, and Pvt's James M. Thrash (21 yrs old) and Leroy N. Thrash (19) were wounded. Other Confederate casualties included Brigadier General Wade Hampton and General Johnston, both severely wounded. From here, President Davis appointed General Lee to command the Confederate Virginia Campaign.

Quotations below by one home writer described experiences the 14th had in the battle and several days previous to it. We believe the writer has two errors. First, the battle at Fair Oaks took place completely south of the Chickahominy, so we believe the statement below "waded across the Chickahominy in a very swampy lowlands" is mistaken. This was more likely a creek in the White Oak Swamp, which feeds into the Chickahominy somewhere west of Fair Oaks. Second, we believe the summation of regimental losses must reflect brigade losses. Our tally from 14th GA Diary is 15 killed and about 50 wounded.

"On Saturday morning, May 24th, needing a break away from the rigors we marched ten miles to Hanover and camped in an old corn field. Next day, we moved over to Long Row Beach and returned to Hanover late that night. On the 26th, we left camp early in the morning and marched ten miles to Cold Harbor. Companies A and B placed on picket duty.

Seven Pines (Fair Oaks)

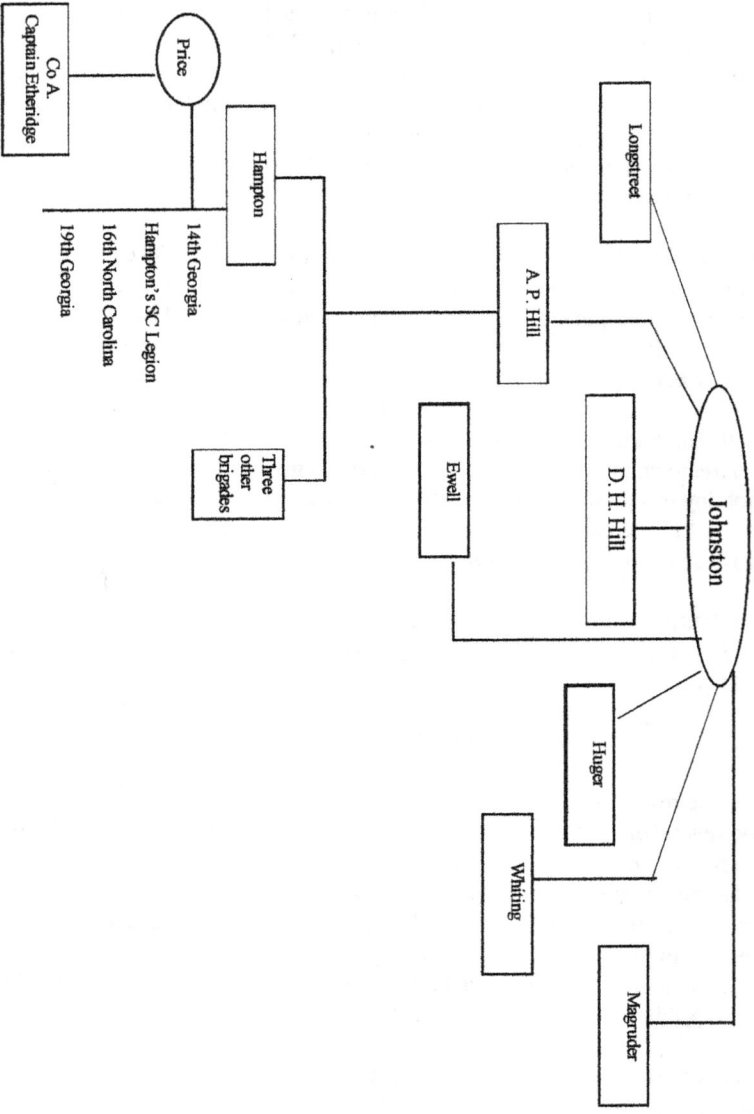

```
                                                                    Longstreet

Co A.          Price          Hampton
Captain Etheridge                                    A. P. Hill
                                                                               Johnston
               14th Georgia                                        D. H. Hill
               Hampton's SC Legion
               16th North Carolina              Ewell
               19th Georgia
                                Three
                                other
                                brigades                                  Huger

                                                                                  Whiting

                                                                                          Magruder
```

Tuesday, May 27th, 1862. We have officially been made a part of A. P. Hill's "Light Division" which means travel light and run fast. Marched over to Ashland. Our mail is a month late; had gone to the 14th Tennessee, then the 14th South Carolina and finally to us. While the mail wagon was parked for pullout in the morning, someone put the torch to the mail wagon, rendering same unmovable. The driver left on bareback leading the second mule to the hoots of everyone awake at the time.

Wednesday, May 28th. Reports on Yankee sightings coming in from every direction. Left camp before daybreak and crossed over the Chickahominy River and marched toward Meadow Bridge. Formed a battle line many times but no attack came. On May 29th, we camped throughout the day and trained for combat. Many attended a Brook's Church revival located nearby. Here we remained in heavy training both days of 29th and 30th of May, 1862. The Yankee army was now forming on the other side of the Chickahominy River from whence we just came.

On Saturday, May 31st, 1862, and long before sunup, our brigade was up and running at 4 AM for perhaps four miles and waded across the Chickahominy River in a very swampy lowland. The idea was to sneak behind a Yankee encampment and attack it on the order of what we accomplished at New Kent Courthouse. It failed to work and they were laying in ambush and served upon us all the minnie balls and cannon grape as hell itself could muster. Double quick time retreat was bugled and back across the swamp went those able to make it. Our company commander, Captain John Etheridge, was shot dead from, and dragged by his horse for a considerable distance. Upon reaching solid ground, we continued to run for over a mile and regrouped with our brigade and attempted to dig trenches before the Yankees were on top of us again. We shifted our position and was ordered to attack a Yankee breastwork on the right flank and here we lay from Saturday until the following Monday afternoon, surviving attack after attack without food, sleep, and little water. We failed to take the breastworks and was relieved by a Virginia led brigade and we retired from the field totally exhausted and the thrills and adventures of war gone from our system forever. Regimental losses 45 killed and 284 wounded. Beyond those officially listed as wounded were multitudes with minor wounds and continued active. Still other wounded were simply left behind in uncontested areas for enemy capture.

THE SEVEN DAYS

By 11 June General Lee had decided that only offensive action to drive off McClellan could save Richmond. A defensive posture against McClellan's superior forces would doom the capital. From JEB Stuart's cavalry reconnaissance, Lee learned McClellan's north flank was vulnerable. His plan called for Jackson to join him (Lee) and to hit McClellan's flank north of the Chickahominy.

In late June McClellan had 60,000 troops facing Richmond south of the Chickahominy and 30,000 troops of Porter's Corps north of the Chickahominy. Lee kept Magruder with only 20,000 troops facing McClellan south of the river, and moved 30,000 troops of A. P. Hill, D. H. Hill, Longstreet, and Ewell north of it. Jackson was expected on the 25th with 20,000 more. Magruder was charged with the task of convincing McClellan that he (McClellan) was faced with a large army south of the Chickahominy. The ruse worked. McClellan wired Washington that he faced 200,000 troops.

Lee planned to destroy Porter's 30,000 north of the river by combined frontal assaults from Ewell, A. P. Hill, D. H. Hill, and Longstreet's divisions with a surprise flank assault from Jackson arriving from the Valley at the last hour. The plan was good, but too complex for Lee's inexperienced army. Jackson had earned a well-deserved reputation as a great combat leader in the Valley and would further secure that reputation at Manassas, Antietam, and Chancellorsville. But the Jackson of the Seven Days was not the leader Lee had hoped for or expected.

At Mechanicsville late in the afternoon of June 26 A. P. Hill's division attacked Porter's V Corps across Beaver Dam Creek near Ellerson's Mill. As described below, the 14th GA was part of the spearhead of this attack. The writer below appears to have Ellerson's (not Ellison's) Mill and Gaines' Mill reversed, however the description is otherwise vivid. The fighting continued for five hours as Hill drove Porter's Corps back 1,200 yards east past the creek at Gaines' Mill. Jackson failed to provide the assault on Porter's north flank, and the US forces escaped destruction. In conversation that evening when Jackson reported, Lee remarked "Ah, General, I am very glad to see you. I had hoped to see you before." This was about as ungentlemanly as Lee's sarcasm ever got.

Over night Porter quietly pulled his forces back east of Gaines' Mill to Cold Harbor. Again in the morning Hill attacked him, only to find empty positions. By 1400, Hill's advance made contact, and his division attacked Porter again, this time across a wide wooded ravine. At 1600, Longstreet joined the attack to Hill's right. At 1630, the divisions of D. H. Hill and Ewell attacked Porter's right. All four attacks were repulsed with heavy losses. But at 1730, Hood's brigade of Longstreet's division broke through the US center. Porter's Corps was in serious trouble, but again Jackson somehow failed to support the attacks with an assault on Porter's north flank.

Lee's plan worked well except for Jackson's sluggish movements. Porter's Corps was very nearly destroyed in the fighting of 27 June at Gaines' Mill. Only darkness saved him. He was able to retreat across the Chickahominy using the dual Grapevine bridges to join the remainder of McClellan's army.

On the night of 27-28 June Lee's five divisions forded the Chickahominy to join Magruder on the south side. At this point two evenly matched armies faced each other, and McClellan elected to give up the plan to take Richmond. US forces began to retreat back toward the James River and to the umbrella of naval gunboats. At sunrise on the 28th Lee's army faced empty U.S. lines.

On the 29th Lee's probing located McClellan's army further east between the Chickahominy and James Rivers. Magruder attacked the US withdrawal at Savage Station on the morning of the 29th. South of the White Oak Swamp, A. P. Hill and Longstreet attacked McClellan on the 30th at Frazer's Farm, routing McCall's division. Incredibly again Jackson failed to hit McClellan's rear to follow up Hill's and Longstreet's victory. The 14th was closely involved in the fierce but indecisive fighting of this day. McClellan continued his withdrawal five miles to Malvern Hill.

On 1 July Lee ordered an assault on the fortified US lines on Malvern Hill. Here the US naval gunboats were able to give the army good protection. D. H. Hill protested Lee's decision to attack Malvern Hill, warning "If General McClellan is in there in strength, we had better leave him alone." Lee insisted, and the infantry assault went forward. Longstreet's and A. P. Hill's exhausted divisions were placed in reserve for this attack. Aaron Jackson's descendants can be grateful for this decision. 5,500 Confederates fell on the slopes of Malvern Hill on 1 July. D. H. Hill later declared "It was not war, it was murder," but McClellan withdrew further to Harrison's Landing, and Lee and Davis could regard Richmond as safe from McClellan's threat.

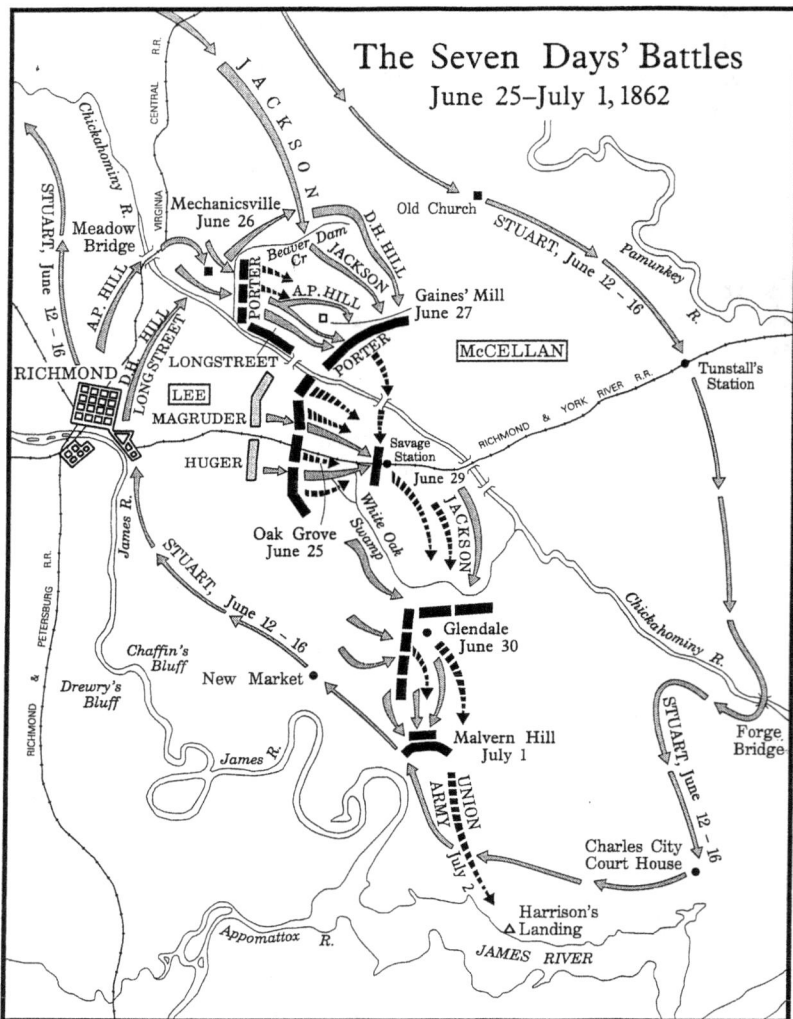

The Seven Days' Battles
June 25–July 1, 1862

AJ's Company A entered the Seven Days fighting with 87 combatants. Colonel Price still had the regiment, and Captain John Mays had command of Company A after Captain Etheridge's death at Fair Oaks. The brigade had been reorganized to include the 14th, 35th, 45th, and 49th GA regiments and the 3rd Louisiana Battalion. Since Brigadier General Hampton's wounds at Seven Pines, Brigadier General Thomas had acting command of the brigade.

In the Seven Days fighting, 2nd Lt. James A. Jordan and Pvt Monroe of Company A were killed at Gaines' Mill on June 27. Company A suffered no further casualties in the Seven Days. The regiment took casualties at Mechanicsville, Gaines' Mill, and Frazer's Farm. In total, the 14th suffered 30 killed and 17 wounded. Letters sent home describe Seven Days from how those in the ranks witnessed it.

"From the 3rd of June 1862 to the 25th we shifted up and down the Chickahominy River's south side near Richmond receiving unaimed scattered cannon shells. We are located not far from the mouth of the James River."

"Thursday, June 26th, 1862. Waded back across the Chickahominy at Meadow Bridge and lined up to do battle near Gaines Mill. In our part of the army's lineup, the 14th Georgia and the 3rd Louisiana Battalion makeup the front column with 35th, 45th, and 49th Georgia Regiments as reserve backup. Around 4 PM, the many bugles sounded the assault and we walked slowly forward driving the Yankee 5th Corps before us taking many prisoners. As backup, the enemy had built ditches and breastworks and it was into these enclaves that the Yankee retreat halted. We continued trying to overrun their positions time and again until 9 PM but without success and the guns fell silent at that time. The artillery on our side moved slowly into position and pounded enemy positions throughout the night allowing little sleep. Grease for our gunlocks was abundantly past around during the late evening hours, which usually meant battle come morning. Yankee artillery was also active throughout the night."

"Friday June 27th before daylight, we deployed three lines deep and our all-out effort began at dawn as everyone present rushed forward with locked bayonets at the signal of our artillery's halt. No one was there. They had pulled out during the night. We went in hot pursuit. On the retreating enemy's road was many wagon loads of dead and wounded Yankee bodies, discarded tents, haversacks, knapsacks, blankets, overcoats, canteens, and wagons of every size. By 10 AM we had advanced to Cold Harbor before receiving serious resistance and here our advance was stopped by a rain of cannon shot. For the remainder of the day and into the night our brigade was locked into mortal combat seldom witnessed on any earthly battlefield. Both sides shot at each other point blank, hand to hand group fights with stick, fists, minnie ball sacks, rocks, and homemade spears. But again God was with us and we survived what was later described as mere rear guard action. The enemy's main body was in full retreat and we are gaining a rich harvest of much needed shoes from Yankee bodies, blankets, medicines and assortment of various weapons left behind."

"On Saturday, June 28th, 1862 we stopped to take care of the wounded and bury the dead. After which we marched to within a half mile of another fight east of Ellison's Mill and leaned on our rifles for several hours, not being allowed to sit down. Lots of dead Yankees and their horses are lying around unburied and we anxiously expected attack at any moment. It never came and after dark we simply slept on the ground with weapons on ready all night. The 45th Georgia, a part of our brigade, was fortunate during this night to have hemmed up and captured a goodly portion of the enemy's 5th Cavalry that had the misfortune of wandering aimlessly into a dead end valley. Monday, June 30th. Up early before daylight and scout reports indicate the enemy is in full retreat back toward Williamsburg. It is in that direction we go encountering some minor rear guard action designed to simply slow us down. Trees were cut in our path and bridges burned or exploded but we continued our march on into the White Oak Swamp area and into camp for preparation for the next morning's all out battle."

"Tuesday, July 1st, 1862. At full daylight, we were ordered into line of battle for the Malvern Hill area. General McGruder inspected our columns and recommended we not be sent on this attack because of the brigade's exhaustion and therefore we were indeed removed and placed to the rear in reserve. But we watched as the battle unfolded before our eyes. The forces of Generals McGruder, Huger, and D. H. Hill pulled out and went on the attack against the entrenched enemy. Both sides lost heavily. But our side faired not as the balance of power was with our enemies. Yankee gunboats on the James River fired their projectiles over the heads of their own army and into our ranks, which proved to be an effective defense and thus we pulled back out of range and broke off the battle. Apart of our army remained on watch but our portion pulled back a distance and into camp. On July 4th while still in camp, we received sixty new recruits. We continued watching the Yankee army and resting until July 8th whereon we broke camp and marched in the direction of Richmond spending considerable time looking for stray Yankees in wooded areas and with some minor success. By Wednesday evening, July 9th, we went back into camp south of Richmond and remained until July 12th at which time we moved to Sassafras, remaining there until Saturday, July 26, 1862."

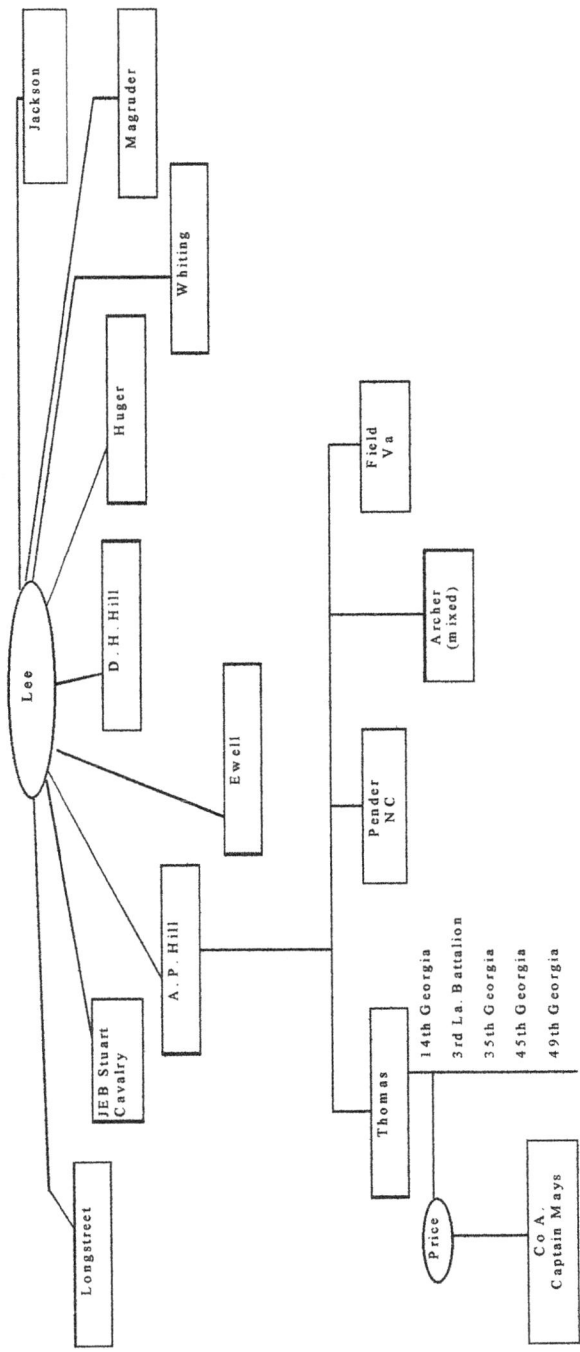

Seven Days

```
                          Jackson

                          Magruder

Lee ──────── Whiting

    ──── Huger

    ──── D.H. Hill

    ──── Ewell

    ──── A.P. Hill ──┬── Field Va
                     │
                     ├── Archer (mixed)
                     │
                     ├── Pender NC
                     │
                     └── Thomas ──┬── 14th Georgia
                                  ├── 3rd La. Battalion
                                  ├── 35th Georgia
                                  ├── 45th Georgia
                                  └── 49th Georgia

    ──── JEB Stuart Cavalry

    ──── Longstreet

Price ──── Co A. Captain Mays
```

SLAUGHTER MOUNTAIN

After the Seven Days battle, Lee attained the first points toward his reputation of the great combat leader he came to acquire. He had saved Richmond against a superior force, but McClellan had inflicted 20,000 casualties on Lee's Army of 90,000. In July McClellan remained camped at Harrison's Landing while General Pope organized an army of 50,000 in Northern VA consisting of Banks' and McDowell's Shenandoah Valley elements. Thus Lee was immediately faced with two strong opponents and at the same time was plagued with a quarrelsome group of senior generals.

After Fair Oaks and the Seven Days, severe arguments developed between Generals Longstreet, Tombs, and A. P. Hill. D. H. Hill became involved in a separate quarrel with Tombs. Lee would be burdened with these difficulties for many months, as would all of the commanders of the Army of Tennessee (Bragg, Johnston, and Hood) for the next years. With the stubborn Bragg it never ended, however Lee was the humble diplomat. His first term solution was to detach D. H. Hill as an independent division away from Longstreet and to send A. P. Hill's division north to join Jackson's Corps. This was a temporary relief for Lee at best, because within days of the move, Jackson and Hill argued, and Jackson placed Hill under arrest. Longstreet remained near Richmond with his newly formed corps, minus D. H. Hill.

On 27 July 1862 Powell Hill's division moved north by rail. Brigadier E. L. Thomas now had command of the Georgia brigade, which included the 14th, 19th, 35th, 45th, and 49th Georgia regiments. These would comprise Thomas' brigade of this division for the rest of the war. Lt. Colonel Felix Price commanded the 14th GA, and Captain Mays continued as Company A's commander, now depleted to 85 men. Recent losses included the deaths of Privates William Goodson, Thomas Hill, John Johnston and Milton Wilson from disease. Four others had been transferred or discharged due to disability. Private Arthur Rucker was enlisted on August 7.

The differences between Generals Jackson and Hill created an open rift that was greater than either of the two leaders could bring himself to heal. Under arrest and disallowed command, Powell Hill struck back by removing his officer's emblems and by walking in the dusty rear of his division in an effort to gain sympathy. Lee ignored the situation, recalling Hill's previous bout with Longstreet and choosing in his silence to support Jackson. But serious as this problem was, it paled in comparison to Lee's deep concerns over the two US armies in Virginia.

22

Cedar Mountain, 2nd Manassas, Antietam Creek, Fredericksburg

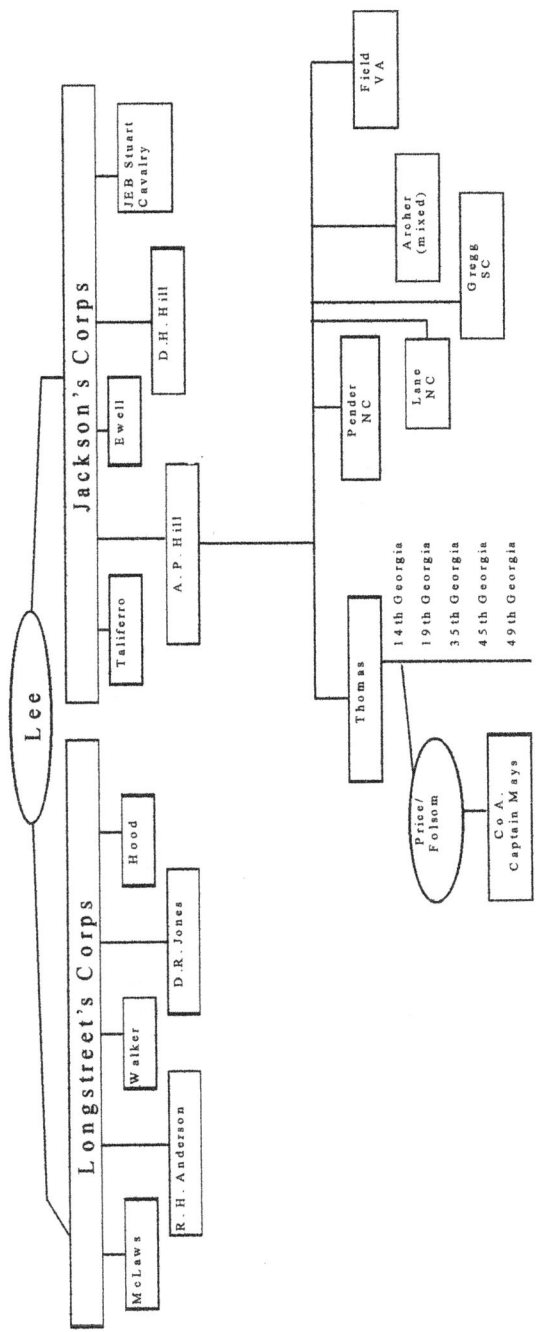

Lee

Longstreet's Corps

- McLaws
- Walker
- R.H. Anderson
- Hood
- D.R. Jones

Jackson's Corps

- Taliferro
- Ewell
- JEB Stuart Cavalry
- D.H. Hill
- A.P. Hill
  - Pender NC
  - Lane NC
  - Archer (mixed)
  - Gregg SC
  - Field VA
  - Thomas
    - 14th Georgia
    - 19th Georgia
    - 35th Georgia
    - 45th Georgia
    - 49th Georgia
    - Price/Folsom
      - Co A. Captain Mays

Against two strong foes, Lee's strategy was to attack Pope in Northern Virginia, reasoning that McClellan would not move against him in the south. Jackson's Corps spearheaded the plan by proceeding against Pope at Cedar Mountain, VA on a very hot Saturday, August 9. The 14th GA joined the battle late in the day in support of several of Jubal Early's Virginia regiments.

Company A suffered one casualty in the wounding of Pvt. Robert Wright at Cedar Mountain, and the regiment suffered seven wounded including Colonel Price, who would resign in October because of his wounds. Jackson won an indecisive victory here. Letters home describe the events at Cedar Mountain (Slaughter Mountain).

"On August 8th, 1862, we are encamped near the Orange County Courthouse. The heat is devastating and stragglers are everywhere to be seen under the shade of trees. August 9th we are bugled from sleep at 2 AM in the morning. In short order we are off and running again. The rumors are wild as to what all this means. The hot temperatures soared from bad to almost unbearable as the day progressed. As evening approached, the sound of cannon could be heard growing closer and closer and written signs along the roadway identify the distant high ground as Slaughter Mountain. Advancing up Culpepper Road, the greater part of our division veered left in support of other units but Thomas' brigade went to the right in support of Early's Virginia brigade, our 14th being absorbed by the 13th, 31st, and 44th Virginia regiments which had suffered many casualties. We positioned behind a wooden fence with a huge cornfield to our front and none too soon as the Yankees burst forth from the woods beyond and came forth toward us in uncountable numbers. Being so ordered, we withheld discharge until our distance was sixty yards and the crash of musketry and artillery cleared the entire cornfield. Immediately afterward, at least a hundred enemy cavalry emerged from the same wooded area and charged our lines with great determination. But our sister regiments had advanced sufficiently to our left to assure a withering crossfire, which wrecked havoc on their advance, which sent horses running in every direction. The enemy infantry on observing the destruction of their cavalry returned to the wooded area and continued their retreat. Our bugles blew double-time forward and we left our hiding places and pursued the retreating army until nightfall to a place called Hudson's Mill. We dug holes and slept by our arms for the remaining portion of the night. Near morning we left the front of the enemy's gathering army and marched back to Slaughter Mountain and begin tending our wounded and burying our own and enemy dead. Sunday, August 10th, 1862- dug trenches preparing for a Yankee attack, which never happened. Everywhere could be seen the scavenging of blue and gray bodies for whatever they might yield. Shoes was always the top item for self and trade. Afternoon brought forth thunder storms with very heavy rains. Monday, August 11th truce granted the Yankees and their wagons entered the area to reclaim the remaining unburied and wounded. Late that evening after the truce teams had departed we piled pine trees along our front lines and fired them to create the illusion of warlike preparations for the following morning; but Jackson had no such intent, and we relocated back across the Rapidan River to improve upon our defenses there. However, no attack came, so we withdrew to move onto the Crenshaw Farm area located between Gordonsville and Orange Courthouse but without tents and slept on the ground and in the open air."

2ND MANASSAS

After Cedar Mountain, Lee began an all-out gamble to defeat Pope, virtually ignoring McClellan. Leaving only token forces opposing McClellan, Lee called Longstreet north to join Jackson. In a huge gamble to trap Pope, he split his army, directing Jackson to march west in a wide sweep through the Bull Run Mountains around Pope. Jackson's Corps of "foot cavalry" marched 62 miles in 48 hours and fell on Pope's supply base at Manassas Junction, 20 miles to Pope's rear. (This feat was but a minor example of Jackson's mobility. His lightening movements here and in the Shenandoah Valley had prompted one of his soldiers to write "his marches started before dawn, except when they started the night before.")

At Manassas Jackson captured valuable U.S. Army stores, including men, cannons, horses, bacon, and corned beef. It is clear from the quotations below that AJ's Company A greatly enjoyed the booty. Jackson's moves initiated the 2nd battle of Manassas. Basically acting as bait, Jackson's Corps moved north to Centerville, then west across Bull Run Creek on the afternoon of the 28th. The next day Jackson started the battle in earnest, though greatly inferior in number. He induced an attack by Pope's Army onto Hill's division. Pope's Army attacked across an embankment of an unfinished railroad bed that forms the extreme northwest edge of what is today designated as Manassas National Battlefield Park. AJ's 14th GA fought all day in close contact with the enemy.

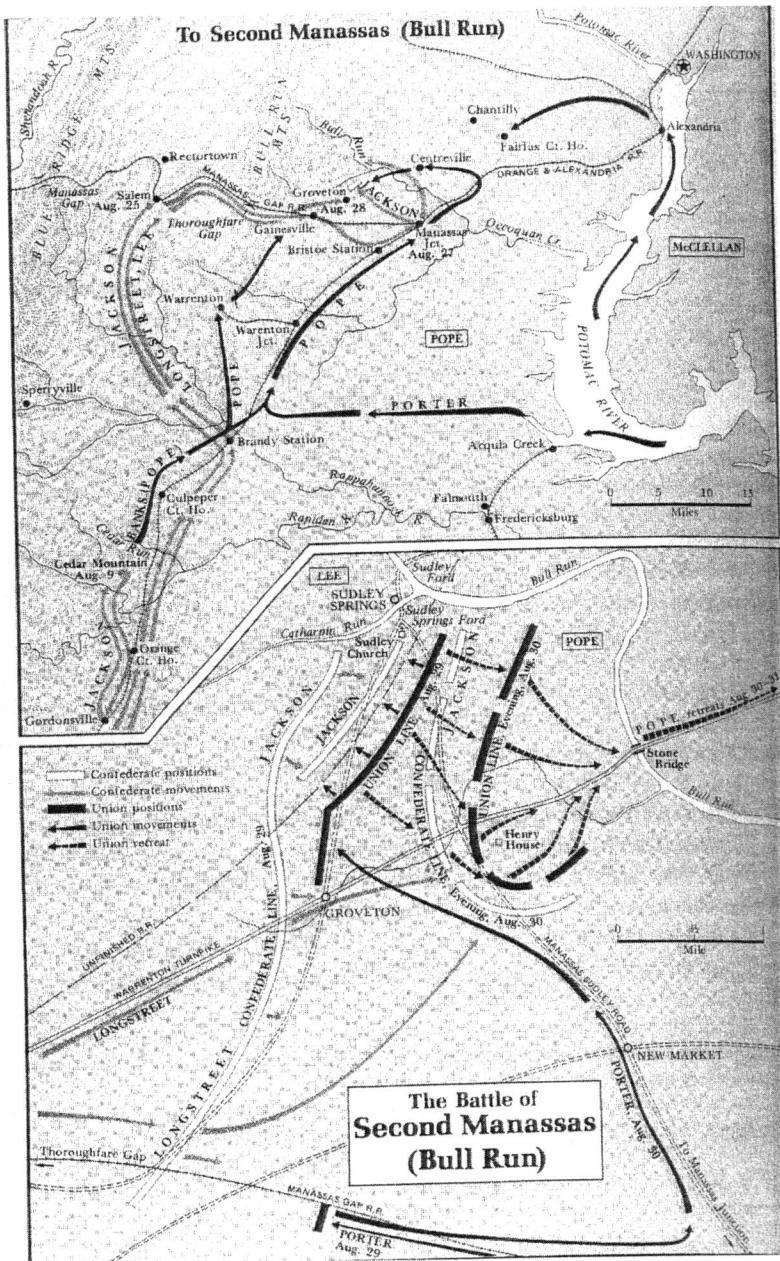

To Second Manassas (Bull Run)

The Battle of
Second Manassas
(Bull Run)

The next day (the 30th), US forces resumed the assault on Jackson. Early in the afternoon, Longstreet appeared on the battlefield, springing the trap almost exactly as Lee had envisioned. Longstreet attacked Pope's left flank in the midst of Pope's assault on Jackson. In the devastation that followed, Hill's division swept the US forces from the field, bending their ends all the way back to Henry House. Here a small force of brave US soldiers held off Hill's division, and Pope's Army was barely able to escape across Bull Run Creek to Centerville.

From Company A Pvt Daniel Perdue and Pvt John Watkins were killed in this fighting. Pvts Benjamin Edge and William Gardener were wounded, but both returned to action. Casualties in the rest of the regiment totaled fourteen. In the account below, the writer home references the killing of U.S. Army General Kearney by the 55th Virginia. This regiment was part of Field's brigade in A. P. Hill's division.

"Friday, August 15th, 1862 - broke camp late in the afternoon and marched northward arriving into camp at Mountain Run with Clark's Mountain in full view to the east of us. The next two days we spent in the most rigid training by General E. L. Thomas heretofore known. He rode from regiment to regiment shouting his disapproval at our performance at Slaughter Mountain. This rebuke was not well received as we had expected handclasps instead of tail kicks. Nevertheless, great respect existed for General Thomas, and his criticism was simply tolerated. Colonel Felix Price is no longer with us because of wounds, and Colonel Robert Folsom, his replacement is now commanding the 14th Georgia infantry. Also we re-dug up Tom Hill, wrapped his body in some Yankee wagon canvas and re-buried him on a hillside overlooking the Rapidan River. Colonel Folsom and others received a special commendation for their performance at the last battle. A gold citation was added to our regimental colors. Six of our brave men were lost and thirty wounded were removed to Richmond East Hospital. August 19th, we underwent no training and instead lounged around and went fishing. August 20th, 1862, we left the area marching northward toward Culpepper and that night camped near Hazel River in the woods near a swamp. Had a pleasant night except for the usual insects and noisy frogs. Two men claimed snakebites. Hunger abounds and marching with only a handful of squash plus wormy corn-on-cob removed from passing fields. This led to excessive irritation in the ranks and fights, which might not have otherwise been. And adding to this is the extreme heat as we trudge along in Virginia's famous red clay dust. But at least it affords the absence of no horsing around from the children soldiers among us. Friday, August 22nd, 1862- up early and the march continues with rain-clouds building overhead and us praying for it to happen. In the afternoon, it did happen and no one complained about walking in it. The conjecture among us is that Jackson has something in mind as there is no slowing the pace. Camped that evening in White Sulphur Springs near a burned bridge. Between us and a large enemy force is General Early's brigade. The bridge needed repair to expedite and make possible Early's escape. We did succeed in those hurried repairs, and General Early was brought to safety complete with cannon and equipment and we cheered when the last member of his army crossed over. The furious enemy rained artillery shells upon us with little effect. August25th- up before daylight and things very much astir. Longstreet's men are coming in by the thousands at quick pace, and we are falling in and moving out with equal dispatch with barely enough time to fill our pockets with green apples and corn ears. Onward through Jeffersontown, Amissville, back across the Rappahanock River, through Orlean and camped late that night near Salem Church. August 26th headed straight east following the Manassas Gap Railroad, which the dusty road generally followed but obstacles along the way would cause the need to cross over at times and back over at other times. After marching for two hours, we went into battle formation at Thoroughfare Gap, but in vain as no enemy appeared. Onward to Haymarket, then Gainesville. Our feet were giving out. Many tied their shoes together and carried them across their shoulders to walk barefooted. Went into camp four miles from Bristoe Station which rumor informs has been successfully overrun by our army. August 27th up very early and marched into Manassas Junction. Fires were everywhere and we made no attempt to put them out. Yankee boxcars were coupled together on sidetracks with many on fire, and yet others had already burnt to their trucks. Still many boxcars had been salvaged and guarded for their content. On some, Jackson's personal guards were literally thrown out of the way and we set about sampling such delicacies unknown and not imagined; that is, champaign, whiskey, spices, coffee, lobster salad, sardines, candy, nuts, fruit juices, pickled pig feet, and things with names not understood. It was truly Christmas in August and all loaded down to the extent that much had to be discarded on the march. August 28th, 1862- bugled awake at one o'clock in the morning with yells that the Yankees are coming, we were in quick formation heading north, but not without our sacks of goodies. We reached Centreville by daylight and observed distant dust clouds from Yankee wagons and infantry. There were no complaints as we began double-timing it westward to rejoin our main army. By early afternoon, we crossed over Bull Run Creek, was involved in a short artillery skirmish, and arrived into Stonewall's ranks before the trap sprang shut. August 29th- Friday starting an hour after daylight, the blue enemy came on wave after wave only to be slaughtered like cattle in front of a railroad embankment which we successfully held. Powder and minnie was soon exhausted with defenders taking advantage of the great abundance of stones seating the railroad ties. Our 14th was front line on top of the embankment and was forced off the top only to be helped back by our sister reserves, and to continue in this tooth and nail fashion until the day's end and honestly thought darkness would never arrive. August 30th the battlefield was quiet somewhat until two o'clock in the afternoon when again the Yankee army came forth three lines deep with banners and in beautiful array as though on a parade field. But as they approached our lines, the artillery from our rear and from Longstreet's unnoticed army devastated the on comers. Their lines became ragged, stunned, and unable to move. And in that state, our bugles blew us forward and we captured a goodly part of Pope's army with the remainder put in full retreat. We pursued them until nightfall when heavy rains began which favored the enemy and rendered forward movement more difficult. August 31st- rain or not, we continued forward throughout the day finding no resistance until the evening of September 1st near Chantilly Plantation near a place called "Ox Hill". Powder was wet on both sides and hand to hand combat became the order of remaining daylight. The lines were uncertain that night and the Yankee General Kearny stumbled in the area occupied by the 55th Virginia and was killed as he attempted escape. The following morning as we went forward, the enemy was gone leaving at least a hundred wagons of equipment."

ANTIETAM CREEK

After the victory at Manassas, Lee decided to take his army north on the offensive. Many historians credited him with reasoning that a Confederate victory in Union territory would likely bring outside assistance from Europe, but it seems unlikely that Lee would be thinking in such political terms. More likely he was thinking tactically and simply wished to inflict a decisive defeat on the US army on Northern soil.

The invasion began in early September, and by the 8th Lee's Army had reached Frederick, Maryland. Here again Lee split his army, sending Jackson west back across the Potomac River. General A. P. Hill, still under arrest and sensing an important battle at hand, appealed to Jackson to reinstate him. On September 11th, Jackson relented and placed Hill back in command of his division.

To open the campaign, Jackson's Corps attacked a smaller force at Harper's Ferry capturing 11,000 prisoners and many supplies. Meanwhile D. H. Hill, with his independent division, became trapped by a far superior US force at South Mountain near Sharpsburg. Here on September 13, Harvey Hill's division stood five divisions of US troops, inflicting heavy casualties. Lee sent his army to rescue Hill's division, and the bloody battle of Antietam Creek ensued.

Jackson's Corps won at Harper's Ferry and in the mid-afternoon of September 15 took off to join the fight at Antietam. Thomas' brigade however remained at Harper's Ferry to guard and parole prisoners and to ship captured supplies back south. In an exciting finish to the bloodiest day of the whole war, A.P. Hill's division (minus Thomas' brigade) hit the Antietam battlefield at 4:30 PM turning an attack from Burnside's Corps away from Longstreet, and saving Lee's Army from worse defeat.

By all accounts Antietam Creek was a US victory. Lee's Army absorbed staggering losses and limped back home across the Potomac. To Lincoln's great fury, McClellan failed to pursue Lee's Army in force. After rejoining the defeated army, Thomas' brigade, along with Gregg's, struck the light enemy pursuit at Shepardstown (today WVA) on September 20, pushing the 118th Pennsylvania back across the Potomac.

Going into the Antietam campaign, Company A of the 14th Georgia contained 83 combat ready troops. In the fighting at Harper's Ferry, Lieutenant Jefferson Hogan was severely wounded and blinded. The regiment suffered no deaths at Harper's Ferry, but suffered three wounded in the September 20 attack at Shepardstown. Letters home pick up immediately after the victory at 2nd Manassas.

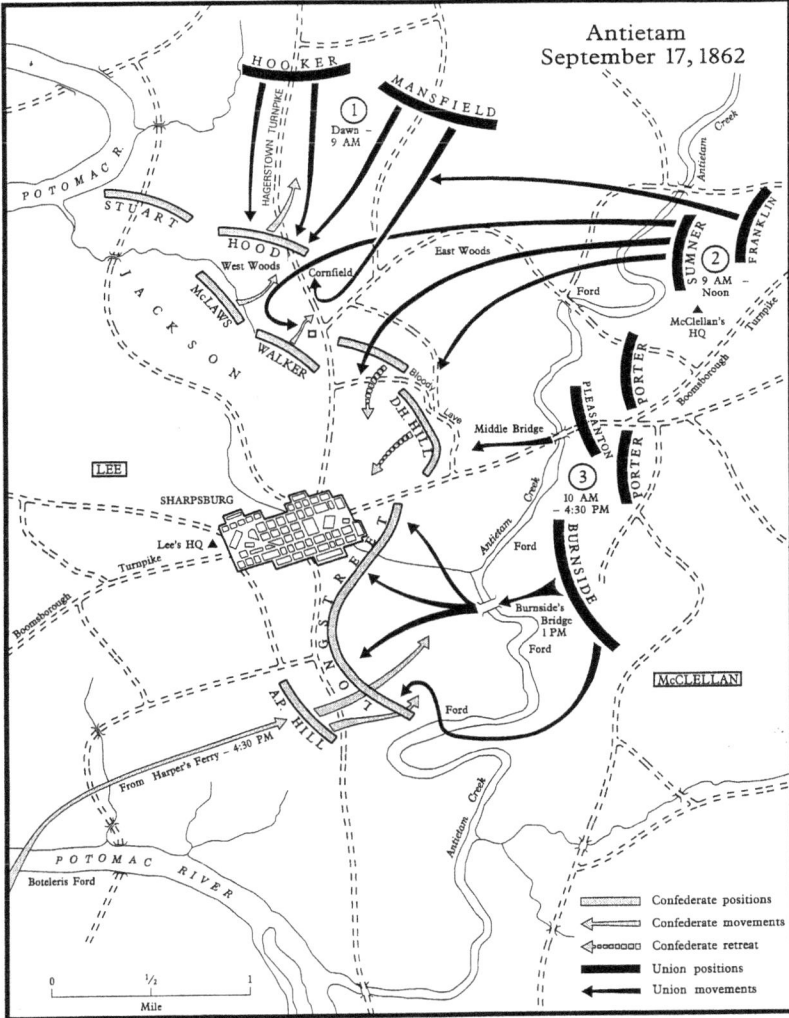

Antietam
September 17, 1862

Legend:
- Confederate positions
- Confederate movements
- Confederate retreat
- Union positions
- Union movements

0   ½   1
Mile

"Saturday, September 6th, 1862 we are walking past the Fairfax County, Virginia, courthouse and General Thomas informs us we are headed into Yankee land. September 7th we cross the Potomac River near Leesburg, and on the 8th we are camping on the outskirts of Frederick City, Maryland. Wednesday, September 10th, General Stonewall Jackson's portion of the army (of which we are a part) departed Frederick City. We left behind a goodly part of the Confederate army, taking a northwesterly line of march and by late afternoon went into camp just outside of Williamsport. Early morning of September 11th, we resume our march heading due south at a rapid pace with our divisional command now back into the reins of A. P. Hill. The disagreement between Generals Hill and Jackson is the talk and worry of the camp. We are in enemy territory and our leaders refuse to speak to one another, so the rumors have it. But this day Hill is back in full uniform and riding up and down the columns to the cheers of some and insults of others. But no matter which side of the argument one found himself, it restored confidence and security to observe him in place. As we continued toward the community of Martinsburg, we crossed the Potomac River at Light's Ford and at this point a part of our army split away westward, but our brigade kept straight down the pike and entered the city in the late hours after dark. The town folks say the Yankee force of only a few thousand had fled eastward toward Harper's Ferry. A few warehouses were loaded with stores of every commodity and what our small army couldn't consume was sent south by wagon train. On September 12th, 1862, we followed the Yankee army eastward. Late in the morning of September 13th, our brigade began forming its battle line on Schoolhouse Ridge and we could see at a distance Yankee infantry doing the same on high ground called Boliver Heights located east of our lines. We skirmished at a distance throughout the evenings with the 9th Vermont who name called us "southern rodents".

But the following day on September 14th brought little action except re-positioning. We followed the Shenandoah banks closer to enemy lines and watched as both sides exchanged artillery shells. So went the day. Monday, September 15th at daylight, the artillery began in earnest and bugles sounded the attack but received no resistance. From the enemy lines came forth a lone Yankee officer carrying a long pole with a white flag. And that ended the Battle of Harper's Ferry and a capture of an enormous cache of powder kegs, a hundred artillery pieces, and over

10,000 enemy soldiers. An entire building of uniforms were exchanged by many of us for the rags and shoes we have been without for the past year. On the evening of the 15th, most of Jackson's army left northward but our brigade was left behind for guard and parole duty. With not enough guards, many of our prisoners escaped. These duties continued through to the evening of the 18th at which time we departed. By midday of the 19th, our brigade had rejoined Jackson's army near Shepherdstown as it returned from Sharpsburg, Maryland. Wagons loaded with the wounded were endless in passing. Insults against Jackson, Longstreet, and Lee were numerous. Our own "Light Division" had fared well and from all accounts had been the saving force at the end of the battle. We gave rearguard to our army who was followed by the 118th Pennsylvania Infantry. We attacked head on, driving the whole of it back into the Potomac River with multitudes being shot crossing the abandoned dam, and still others as they swam back across. With the coming of a large Yankee force, we retired southward and camped near Bunkersville located not far from Winchester, Virginia. Here we remained, regrouping, training new recruits, and resting in general. October 28, 1862, broke camp and marched to a point near Berryville and remained near Castleman's Ferry until November 10th. Stonewall Jackson had enjoyed our railroad damage last month and sent us here to accomplish more of it, and so we proceeded to tear up Yankee track for at least twenty-five miles."

FREDERICKSBURG

The story of the battle of Fredericksburg can scarcely be told from the perspective of any Confederate Army unit. It is a story that should be told from the perspective of the Army of the Potomac, which attained its nadir of administrative performance in the days preceding the battle, and whose leadership during the battle cost the casualties of thousands of superb soldiers. Unfortunately for any writer, Bruce Catton has describe this period in his book Glory Road with such entertaining skill, that there remains very little hope of adding any useful prose to the subject.

From the start of the war up through at least Chancellorsville the soldiers of the Army of the Potomac never received leadership worthy of them. The contributions to this sorry state of leadership made during the Fredericksburg-Mudmarch campaign did however result in observable improvements in the Army. Of the soldiers on the roles of the Army of the Potomac from the Peninsula

Campaign up through Fredericksburg, most no longer appeared. Losses from sickness, combat casualties, desertions, and refusal to re-enlist amounted to about two-thirds of the original army. But of the third that remained, these men could stand up to a great deal of beating. Of this third Meade and Grant would in the later months identify junior officers and NCOs with which they would be able to win the war. So it might even be that the blundering and losses at Fredericksburg were the necessary school required for this army to beat Lee and his superior generals.

Major General Ambrose Burnside attained command of the Army of the Potomac on November 9, 1862, and immediately submitted a plan to put it in motion to attack Lee. Lincoln approved the plan with the admonishment that Burnside would succeed only if he moved quickly. Unfortunately Burnside had the enthusiastic support of neither his superior Halleck nor of his subordinates, and he did not possess the fortitude to light a fire under his subordinates to attain the fast action required.

When Burnside ascended to command, he had no expectation to fight a battle at Fredericksburg. He intended for Major General Sumner's two corps of infantry to cross the Rappahannock at the fords north of Fredericksburg and to occupy it and Marye's Heights west of town. Then the rest of the army including artillery, infantry, and cavalry with their logistics support would cross the river unopposed at Fredericksburg on pontoon bridges. By November 17, Sumner was in position with his 40,000 men to ford the Rappahannock to occupy Fredericksburg, and by the 19th Hooker was ready with another 40,000 opposite Fredericksburg to cross the river as soon as the pontoon bridges appeared.

On the 19th both Sumner and Hooker could have crossed the river unopposed by Lee, and Burnside could have done his fighting south and west of the Rappahannock as planned. On the 19th Lee ordered a division of Longstreet's Corps to occupy Fredericksburg and Marye's Heights, but they were not there yet, and Sumner could still easily beat them there. Unfortunately the pontoon bridges required for Hooker's crossing were still in northern Maryland and were slowly being transported to Fredericksburg by Major Ira Spaulding and the men of the 50th New York Engineers. And so Burnside and Sumner politely sat on the banks of the Rappahannock and waited for Spaulding to arrive.

Spaulding's orders included no sense of urgency, and neither Burnside nor any subordinate between him and Spaulding made any significant move to speed the arrival of the bridges. The 50th Engineers worked very, very hard to get the pontoon bridges over the impossible roads to Fredericksburg even without being aware of why they were so urgently needed there. So no blame can be placed on these men for holding up Burnside's operation, and anyway, they would be among the first to die when the delay evolved into the battle of Fredericksburg.

On the 19th Burnside might have ordered Sumner across on the gamble that Sumner could hold his "beachhead" for as long as it took to obtain and construct the pontoon bridges. But it would have been a huge gamble. If November rains should raise the river level to make the fords impassable after Sumner crossed and before the pontoon bridges were in place, Lee would have the perfect opportunity to destroy one third of the Army of the Potomac while Burnside watched helplessly from the opposite bank of the Rappahannock.

With the Army of the Potomac on that opposite bank, Lee moved Longstreet's entire corps to Marye's Heights behind Fredericksburg. By November 24, what was once an excellent plan to attack Lee, was no longer a good plan at all. The bridges were still days away, and all of Burnside's Army was still on the east bank of the Rappahannock. When the bridges finally arrived on 8 December, Burnside considered his next move. His options were 1) to cancel the operation, 2) to move north or south to outflank Lee and cross elsewhere, 3) to feign a direct crossing at Fredericksburg and move north or south, or 4) to mount a frontal assault river crossing at Fredericksburg against a hostile force. Bruce Catton describes Burnside's decision in his book entitled Glory Road:

"Burnside, after sitting there bemused for three weeks had finally come to a decision. It seemed to him now that the enemy would be more surprised by a crossing right at Fredericksburg than by a crossing at any other place, and in a way he was right. Probably nothing in all the war surprised Lee quite as much as the discovery that his enemy would move up for a frontal assault at Fredericksburg, although this was not a surprise that gave the Federal's any military advantage. In any case, on December 9th Burnside called the Grand Divisional Commanders to headquarters and instructed them to have their commands ready to move at daylight on December 11th. To Major Spaulding, Burnside sent word to stand by: the army was at last ready to use those pontoons."

On the cold foggy morning of 11 December the 50th New York Engineers began stretching their three pontoon bridges across the river toward Fredericksburg. The sounds were unmistakable in the darkness, and Lee moved Barksdale's brigade of Mississippi riflemen into town to pick off the bridge builders. Lee also sent for Jackson's Corps from the Valley to join him in Fredericksburg. This brought A. P. Hill's division and the 14th GA to the scene. As daylight broke on the 11th

35

Barksdale's riflemen began killing the helpless engineers of the 50th New York. Infantry from the east bank tried to support the engineers, but as they built closer to the Fredericksburg shore, Barksdale's men had all of the advantages. After three aborted attempts to complete the pontoon bridges, US artillery were given the order to level the town of Fredericksburg. This the artillery accomplished, but Barksdale's brigade "taught the lesson which artillerists have to learn anew in each generation – a bombardment which will destroy buildings will not necessarily keep brave defenders from fighting on in the wreckage" (Catton, Glory Road, pg. 49). The 50th Engineers trotted out on the bridges again "but the pinpoints of flame sputtered again from [the Fredericksburg wreckage], and more engineers were shot down, and once again it was too hot to build bridges." (Catton, pg 49).

The solution to the problem was derived by three regiments of infantry. The 7th Michigan and the 19th and 20th Massachusetts regiments were loaded onto Major Spaulding's pontoons to use as assault boats to rush the opposite bank. This brigade of US infantry was composed of very brave men who demonstrated a very strong desire to win this war at great personal sacrifice. The three regiments obtained a foothold on the Fredericksburg side and then with heavy losses cleared the town in door to door fighting. At the end of the day of the 11th Burnside had possession of Fredericksburg and could put his troops across as he pleased.

Burnside spent the day of the 12th getting the greatest portion of his army across the river and in position to assault Lee. But securing the foothold and getting his army across turned out to be the minor dangers the Army of the Potomac would face at Fredericksburg. And this is where A. P. Hill's light division, Thomas' Georgia brigade, and the 14th GA regiment impacted the battle on the 13th greatly and pushed Burnside into a decision that would nearly destroy the Army of the Potomac.

By the end of the 12th Lee had Longstreet's Corps occupying Marye's Heights above and west of Fredericksburg and Jackson's Corps stretching south of town towards Hamilton's Railroad crossing, as seen on the Fredericksburg map. A. P. Hill's division was located on the right end of Jackson's line, which lay before and behind the Richmond railroad tracks. The US plan was for Franklin's Grand Division of two excellent corps to attack Jackson's Corps to break through at Hamilton's Crossing in order to outflank Lee at Fredericksburg and then to roll the line up northward while Sumner frontally assaulted Marye's Heights. The plan was a good one if things had gone right. In fact A. P. Hill's portion of the line probably was the weak spot, and Franklin's attack almost made Fredericksburg a US victory instead of the worst defeat in U.S. Army history.

On the morning of the 13th Thomas' brigade was near the middle of A. P. Hill's section of Jackson's line. The brigade occupied high ground above and behind the railroad tracks in support of the Pender and Lane brigades, who held the front. A. J.'s Company A entered the fighting with 81 soldiers ready for combat. Colonel Folsom led the regiment, and Captain Mays commanded Co. A. These men of Hill's division would bear the brunt of Franklin's attack and would absorb 50% of all Confederate casualties at Fredericksburg and 40% of all Confederate deaths.

Franklin's attack momentarily crumbled Lane's and Pender's brigades and cut the railroad line. But then Thomas' brigade rushed in to recapture the tracks and to smash the US assault on this portion of the battlefield. The action of Thomas' brigade is cited today on the Fredericksburg battlefield placards placed on Lee Drive extending south toward Hamilton's Crossing.

When this portion of the attack failed to break Hill's and Jackson's line, the US assault concentrated in the afternoon of December 13 on Marye's Heights. Here "the Yankees were with power, but in all the war the Southerners never had to worry as little about a battle as about this one"(Catton, pg 53). On this portion of the field Longstreet's Corps was ready with all of the advantages. The US troops had to advance uphill over a plain on which a Confederate gunner had assured Longstreet not even a chicken could live. Longstreet subsequently promised Lee "to kill every man in the Union Army, provided his ammunition held out."

If the US II Corps had tried, it could not have found a worse place than Marye's Heights to make an attack. The men of this corps were veterans, and they knew a bad spot when they saw it. And so the valor the fourteen brigades displayed in their 14 separate assaults on Marye's Heights can never be exaggerated. The attacks had to be made over 400 yards of open uphill terrain. This terrain was narrowed by natural obstacles, so that only a brigade at a time could make the assault. Each brigade was attacking the whole of Longsteet's Corps, which had formed a line behind a four-foot stone wall placed before a wide sunken road – "as invulnerable a trench as the rebels could have found in the whole state of Virginia." (Catton, pg 62).

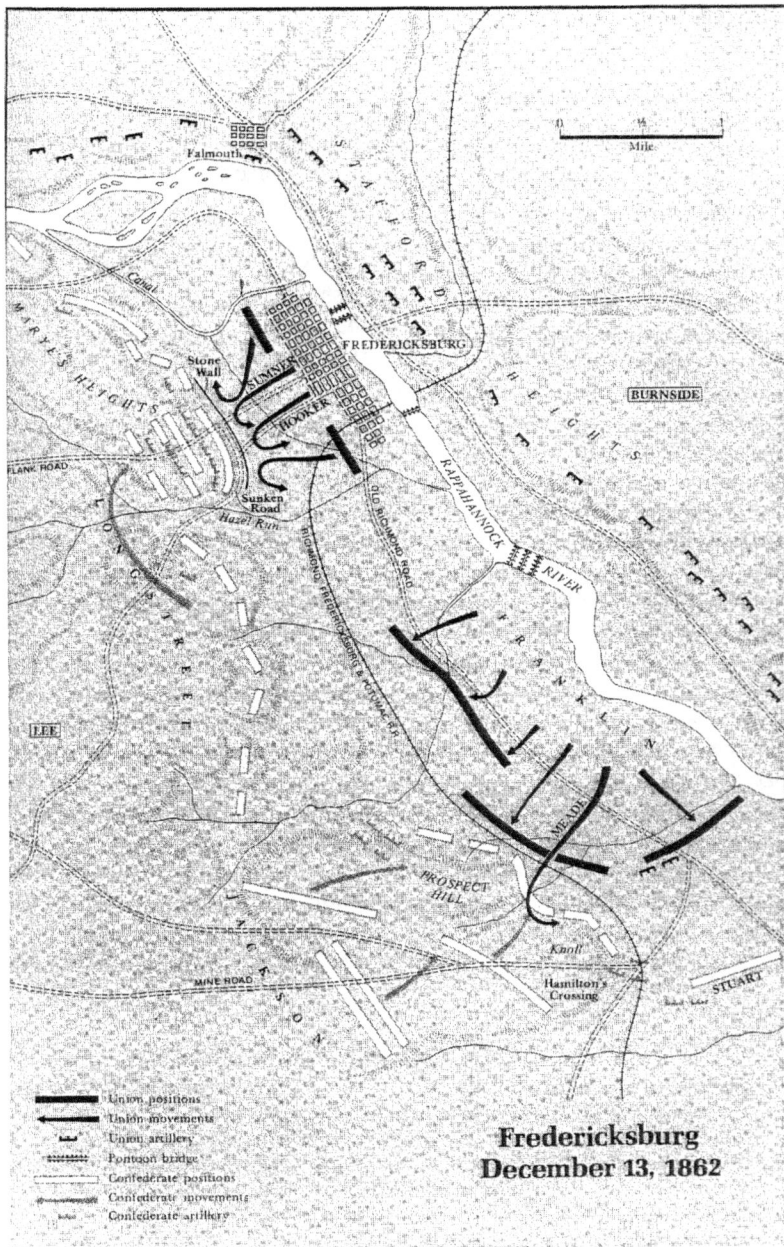

Fredericksburg
December 13, 1862

Union positions
Union movements
Union artillery
Pontoon bridge
Confederate positions
Confederate movements
Confederate artillery

The attacks on Marye's Heights were complete folly. Almost every brigade involved absorbed greater than 50% casualties, and most inflicted negligible losses on the defending Confederates. After Kimball's division of three brigades completed the first assaults it looked to the Confederates on the heights as though the plain had turned blue with US bodies. The fourth brigade to attack suffered 1,150 casualties out of 1,400 men. In the sixth brigade to attack, the 5th New Hampshire regiment lost four successive commanders in ten minutes. Divisions from the III, V, and IX Corps joined the fight with no different results.

In the mid-afternoon Hooker was ordered to attack with his division of two brigades from the V Corps. Hooker was known in the army as fightin' Joe Hooker, and despite his later performance at Chancellorsville that is what he was. But today even Hooker was reluctant. "He consulted Crouch and Hancock, and from them learned the desperate character of the onslaught. The plain was already filled with dead and wounded. Burnside should know about that, so Hooker rode two miles to Burnside's headquarters to tell him it was no use to try to carry that line. But Burnside was obdurate. (Near twilight) Hooker sent his two brigades over the same ground already covered with the fallen, and added to the heaps of dead." (Hansen, The Civil War) One of these two brigades suffered 140 casualties and never was able to get in position to fire a shot at the enemy. The last attack was made by Hawkin's brigade from IX Corps in almost complete darkness.

How could General Burnside order these attacks on so impregnable a position? He was under no desperate condition and could easily and intelligently have waited for more favorable circumstances. US generalship was terrible, but the significant thing about the endless succession of doomed assaults across the Fredericksburg plain was not that a stupid general ordered them, but rather that the army which had to make them had never once faltered. "The story of Fredericksburg comes down at last to a simple accounting of the bravery which men can display and the price that can be extracted when they do display it, and if the men gain anything at all by any part of it, there is a transcendental scale of values in operation which it would be nice to know about." (Catton)

"And yet this disastrous fight, as barren of concrete results as any battle the Army of the Potomac ever fought, was nevertheless in its own tragic way a dim beacon of light for the future." For the tradition of heroism this army set at Fredericksburg would live for the rest of the war, and the third that remained would show itself to be a formidable opponent. From here Lee's Army knew that the Army of the Potomac was a fierce and determined one filled with soldiers that would fight and die. Any victories won over this huge and competent army would be won only by an opposing force that was very good.

Recall that in the Fredericksburg fight A. P. Hill's division bore the dominant share of Confederate casualties. The 14th GA shared completely in the distribution. The regiment suffered 24 killed and 71 wounded in the fighting to re-establish control of the Richmond railroad, for a casualty rate approaching 20%. Company A lost Pvts. William Holland, Ichabod Mitchell, and Walter Thomas killed and Cpl Jerry Lumpkin mortally wounded. Captain Mays was also wounded, but remained on duty. Thomas's men had performed well, and a member of the 14th Georgia claimed in a letter home that Colonel "Cedar Run" Folsom, was "the proudest man I ever saw of his Regiment." The eyewitness account picks up shortly before Jackson's move to Fredericksburg.

On November 20th, we moved to another camp a mile north of Camp Lee. Two days later, we broke camp and marched through Kernstown, Middletown, and went into camp late in the afternoon at New Town, Virginia. November 23rd, we marched hard and fast passing through Strasburg and in the early afternoon went into camp near Woodstock. Due to the snow and ice, we went into the woods gathering pine straw to pile onto the ground for bedding. On Monday, November 24th, 1862, broke camp long before daylight and past through Woodstock, Hawkstown, Edinburg, and went into camp just beyond. Tuesday, November 25th we past through Mount Jackson, New Market, crossed the Shenandoah River, and went into camp at the foot of a spur near Swift Run Gap. On Wednesday, November 26th we continued to cross the mountains and camped that evening at Fisher's Gap. November 27th, we completed our crossing of the Blue Ridge Mountains and camped on the eastside. On Saturday, November 29th, continued our march and in the early evening camped at Orange County Courthouse. On Sunday, November 30th left before daybreak and that evening camped near Orange Springs. By December 2nd, we camped near Guiney's Station. And finally, our journey somewhat ended the following day, December 3rd when we marched onto Military Road and a short march later, into some thick woods five miles south of Fredericksburg, Virginia. We had been on a continuous march for the past twelve days after leaving camp north of Winchester. Perhaps we had covered during this time frame around two hundred miles and over some of the most appalling terrain on the face of God's earth and through weather, such as rain, snow, sleet, and any other condition one can possibly nightmare up. The weather turned against us on December 4th and 5th with snow generally five inches deep and snow drifts up to four feet. Shoes, clothing, and especially overcoats were lacking with almost everyone. The suffering among us is indescribable. We shifted our camp onto an area called Yerby's Farm. On December 10th, the weather improved and we moved into battle position, it now being clear that Lee expected the Yankees in a big way and thus the purpose for the unbelievable hard march.

On Thursday, December 11th, 1862, we are located just off Military Road digging our trenches, or as some put it "our graves". The Pender and Lane brigades are on the other side of this same road facing the Richmond, Fredericksburg, and Potomac Railroad. Most simply call the railroad, "the Richmond tracks." Our Brigade is also located one mile north of Hamilton's Crossing, and nearby Flattop Hill is called "Prospect Hill" on top of which some of our top officers will gather to review Yankee progress. The Yankees are busy bees floating lots of boats, connecting them, and building bridges on top of the floating boats in order to cross the river. Our many units of artillery are in place but not shooting. One such placement under a Major Walker is situated with fourteen pieces off to our right. The gathering storm is at the moment being taken by our side with great calm. Gambling continues unabated into the wee hours. The three very pretty New Market girls are packing to leave as they sense the rising tension. They were the talk of the camp and perhaps the object of a forth. On Friday, December 12th is spent aiding Major Walker to level his cannon areas and also dig trenches for powder storage. Also we fill up pickle barrels with dirt and roll them into place around the artillery compound. Ike and Tom Mitchell return from helping to shoot at Yankee bridge builders and inform us that the City of Fredericksburg has fallen and is now occupied by uncountable hordes of enemy troops."

"Daybreak reveals a heavy fog, but as the morning progressed, this gradually faded and mostly gone by mid-morning at which time a thunderous yell is heard from the enemy's side and their expected attack is underway. Major Walker's fourteen artillery pieces start their shoot rendering great frustration in talking or listening. In short order things were tooth and nail with minnie balls and enemy shells falling in great abundance. The Pender and Lane brigades to our front were being overrun and our brigade was bugled forward in double-time fashion in support of our sister brigades. As a result we pushed forward into their ranks, and it became a Pender-Thomas brigade and thus unified we devastated Yankee onrushes. Jubal Early's brigade also shifted placing the enemy in a horrible crossfire. The Walker artillery battery is fast dumping bucketfuls of nuts and bolts into cannon mouths which multiply enemy dead and wounded into piles of mangled human carnage. Certainly half of the attacking enemy lay dead or dying before our lines and those fortunate enough to escape in retreat did not again return. Our portion of the line was secure by two-thirty o'clock in the evening but we could hear constant cannon and rifle fire to the north of us before General Longstreet's front. We continued in our trenches unattacked throughout the balance of the evening even until 9 PM when relieved by Early's Virginia regiments and we departed exhausted and suffering under a chorus of enemy moans from their wounded laying unattended on the battlefield and their screams growing into a united wail which seem to grow louder, ghostlike, and profoundly nerve-racking and there was no rest or sleep until we moved out of hearing. At 4 AM on the morning of 14 December 1862 we moved back into the trenches and continued throughout the day expecting a renewal of battle which came not. After Christmas we moved south and followed the river down stream perhaps twenty miles and began building a large fort complete with breastworks of sorts. This was called "Camp Gregg" and it was here we settled into winter quarters and ultimately a four month stay to almost the end of April, 1863."

CHANCELLORSVILLE

Lee's Army spent the winter and early spring encamped near Fredericksburg training for the summer campaign. A. P. Hill's division spent January assisting the citizens of Fredericksburg to recover from the recent battle. It is not obvious whether this would be considered good duty or bad, but it is clear the troops of the 14th GA did not prefer it. The dispute from July 1862 between Jackson and Hill was still on-going, and many might have considered this assignment another punitive measure taken by Jackson against Hill. The troops of Hill's division were used to the perception of getting the ass end of Jackson's decisions. Whatever Jackson's reasoning in this assignment, Hill's division was glad in February to join the bulk of Lee's Army at Camp Gregg, several miles south of Fredericksburg. From then until mid-April the army spent a winter of bivouac boredom – combat training, picket duty, artillery practice, drill, inspection, and passes with little entertainment.

By the coming spring campaign Hooker had relieved Burnside as commander of the Army of the Potomac and had in excess of 120,000 ready troops to defeat Lee. Lee had sent Longstreet's Corps (minus McLaw's division) to forge for the army in North Carolina and to confront any US thrusts from the Hampton-Yorktown region. Thus Lee had only 53,000 troops to face Hooker's far larger army. Hooker grasped the initiative and completely outmaneuvered Lee to start the spring fighting.

Leaving Lt. General Sedgwick with 40,000 troops east of the Rappahannock to confront Lee's 53,000 at Fredericksburg, Hooker sent 10,000 cavalry south on a raid and marched 70,000 infantry up the Rappahannock, crossing to the south of it at Ely's Ford. With much of Lee's cavalry occupied by Hooker's cavalry, Hooker was able to approach Lee's rear near Chancellorsville. By the evening of April 30, Hooker had his army of 70,000 troops in position east of Chancellorsville, completely surprising Lee.

On May 1, Lee realized the extremity of his position, facing an army of 40,000 to his immediate east and an army of 70,000 to his immediate west, and was forced into one of his boldest gambles. Against West Point doctrine, Lee divided his army. Leaving Early with only 10,000 men to face Sedgwick's 40,000, Lee moved west with 43,000 to battle Hooker's 70,000. The two armies clashed in minor skirmishing in the open country east of Chancellorsville late on May 1. Surprisingly and much to the dismay of several of his corps commanders, Hooker pulled back from this open country into the Wilderness woods near Chancellorsville. With this move he gave up much of the tremendous advantage his flanking march had given him. The dense Wilderness woods partly neutralized the advantage he had in infantry and artillery.

On the night of May 1, Lee and Jackson made plans for what remains one of history's greatest combat gambles. Outnumbered almost two to one, Lee would outflank and attack his opponent. The plan was almost entirely Jackson's, and Lee allowed him to determine its execution.

At the dawn of May 2, Jackson began a flanking march with his entire corps of 30,000 men, leaving Lee with only 13,000 troops to face Hooker. Jackson's march of about twelve miles took his corps first south on the Catherine Furnace Road, then west, and finally north on Brock Road to the Orange Turnpike. The march left Lee's tiny force in great peril from frontal attack by Hooker for the next twelve hours. A. P. Hill's division moved out last in Jackson's movement with Brigadier General Thomas' brigade departing about 1100.

CHANCELLORSVILLE

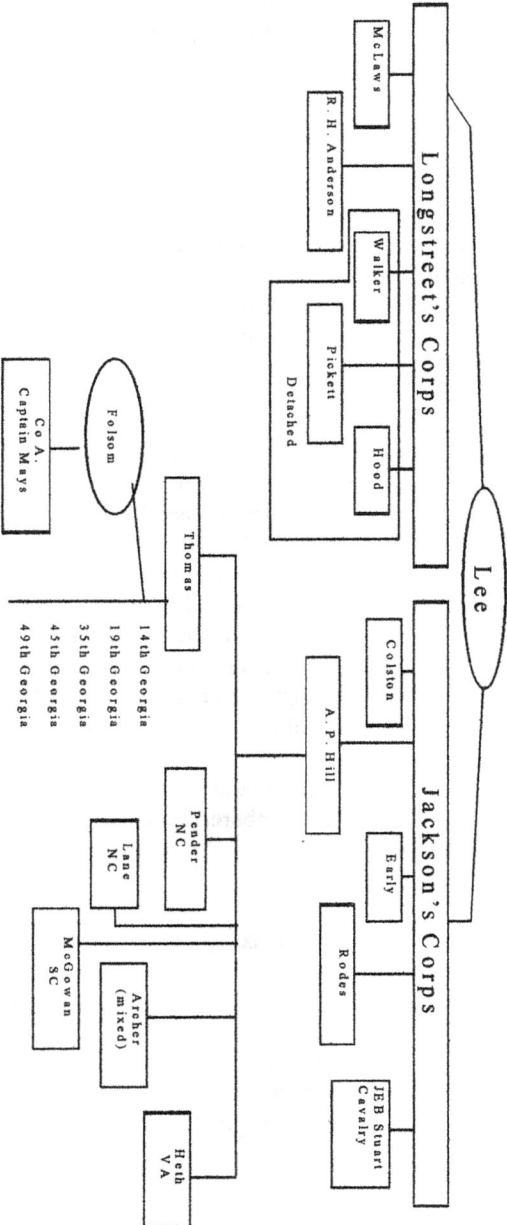

Lee

Longstreet's Corps

- McLaws
- R. H. Anderson
- Walker
- Pickett
  - Detached
- Hood

Jackson's Corps

- A. P. Hill
  - Colston
  - Pender NC
    - Lane NC
    - McGowan SC
    - Archer (mixed)
    - Heth VA
- Early
- Rodes
- JEB Stuart Cavalry

- Thomas
  - Folsom
    - Co A. Captain Mays
  - 14th Georgia
  - 19th Georgia
  - 35th Georgia
  - 45th Georgia
  - 49th Georgia

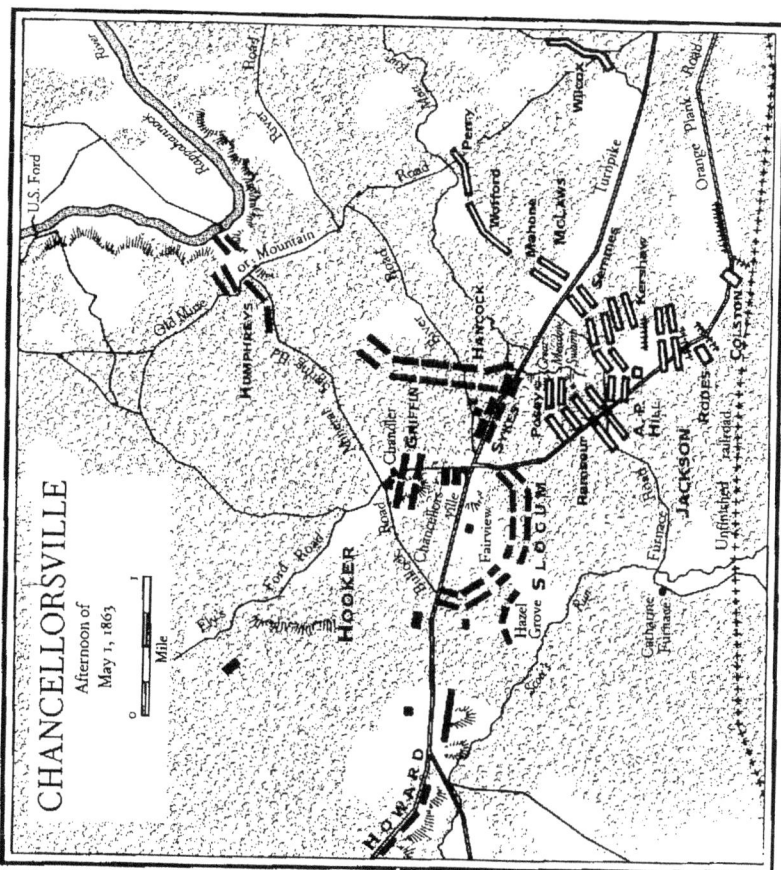

CHANCELLORSVILLE
Afternoon of
May 1, 1863

This tail end of the movement was discovered and attacked by Major General Sickles' division. Brigadier Generals Thomas and Archer's brigades were forced to double back to counter this attack. Sickles' infantry took several prisoners from the 23rd GA regiment, but Hooker failed to recognize Jackson's movement as a flanking maneuver. He assumed it was a retreat, and did not assault Lee's front.

By 5:10 PM Jackson's Corps was in position to attack, facing east on the Orange Turnpike. The flanking gamble had succeeded brilliantly. Jackson's two-mile front faced the exposed right flank of Lt. General Howard's XI Corps. Howard's Corps was dug in parallel to the Orange Turnpike, facing south. Jackson attacked along a two mile front which was three divisions deep, completely routing Howard's Corps. As events evolved, Thomas' and Archer's brigades had not been able to rejoin Hill's division in time for this attack, but even without them Jackson drove the US forces two miles down the turnpike and turned their front to face west. The attack was speared by BG Rodes' division. Colston's division formed the second rank, and A.P. Hill's division formed the third rank.

At the sound of battle Lee attacked along his front also, and the battle raged into the morning hours of 3 May, thus developing into one of the war's rare night actions. At 2100 A.P. Hill's division moved up to the front of Jackson's Corps, relieving Rodes' division after the initial assault. Archer and Thomas were just then approaching the front.

Just after 2100 that evening Jackson and Hill personally reconnoitered between the lines of the two armies. Upon returning to the Confederate lines, the party was fired on by Lane's North Carolina brigade of Hill's division. Jackson fell mortally wounded. A.P. Hill, the senior Major General of the corps, took command of the front. Within minutes he too would be painfully wounded in the calf. Command descended to Brig. Gen. Rodes. Rodes soon yielded to Major General Stuart who took command of the front about 0200. Within the space of several hours Jackson's Corps had changed command three times.

With Hill wounded, Heth assumed command of Hill's six brigades in the hours after midnight. He extended them over the front stretching almost two miles across the Orange Turnpike from north to south in the order of Thomas, Pender, Lane, McGowan, and Archer with Brockenbough (Heth's brigade) in reserve behind Pender and Lane. Stuart arrived at Heth's front shortly before dawn and without instructions from Lee or Jackson knew instinctively Lee's intentions to attack. At 0500 3 May, Heth's entire front jumped off in the first wave of what would become a day of the war's hardest fighting.

Even after Jackson's brilliant success of the previous day, Hooker was still in good position to win the battle. Lee's front was still greatly out manned. On Heth's front the Confederates attacked two US divisions that were well dug in and waiting. After initial gains of one mile, most of the front was then counterattacked and thrown back. Stuart threw in Colston's division in a second wave and then Rodes' division in a third wave of attack. All three divisions were badly mauled, suffering 6,800 casualties. The attack resulted in close combat in which Heth's (Hill's) division suffered 22% casualties including three general officers. Lane's brigade alone took 909 casualties. Thomas' brigade on the extreme left of Heth's line suffered the lightest casualties of the division, but clearly the 14th was in very hard fighting. Of the 50 companies engaged under Thomas, Company A of the 14th GA suffered one-seventh of the brigade deaths that day.

By 9 AM the Confederate front was one-fourth mile further back than where Heth had started at 5 AM, and the troops were cowering under US artillery. Thomas' northernmost flank was badly exposed to both Reynold's and Meade's Corps. Both commanders separately requested permission to attack this flank and were denied permission. Hooker had missed another golden opportunity.

At 10 AM Lee attacked his front and instructed Stuart to fight his way through his right to reunite with Lee. Both generals were successful, and they were able to push Hooker's Army out of Chancellorsville. Confederate artillery firing from Hazel Grove was instrumental in the day's results. US forces were driven north to form a horseshoe-like line anchored on the Rapidan and Rappahannock Rivers.

This same day Sedgwick attacked west from Fredericksburg. His corps finally over-ran Early's division after three assaults on the same battlefield as of 13 December. Early fell back, sending riders the nine miles to inform Lee that he had an army of 40,000 approaching his rear. Lee sent McLaws' division and then Anderson's to assist Early to halt Sedgwick near Salem Church, about halfway between Fredericksburg and Chancellorsville. This left only Stuart's Corps of 26,000 to face the remains of Hooker's 70,000. After two days of retreat and defeat, Hooker was still in good position to attack from both his and Sedgwick's fronts and to crush Stuart and Lee. Instead he ultimately withdrew all corps north of the Rappahannock and broke off contact. At the end of the battle Lee moved back to Fredericksburg, and Hooker and Sedgwick rejoined north of the Rappahannock.

CHANCELLORSVILLE

Afternoon of
May 2, 1863

48

Chancellorsville was probably the Confederate Army's most brilliant performance. Quoting from Mcpherson, Battle Cry of Freedom, "By any standard he [Lee] had won an outstanding victory, recognized as such in both North and South. Without Longstreet and with little more than half as many men as an enemy who had initially outmaneuvered him, Lee had grasped the initiative, gone over to the attack, and had repeatedly divided and maneuvered his forces in such a way as to give them superiority or equality of numbers at all points of attack. The exhausted but exultant rebels, who had fought with an elan unprecedented even in this victorious army, cheered wildly as Lee rode into the clearing around the burning Chancellorsville mansion."

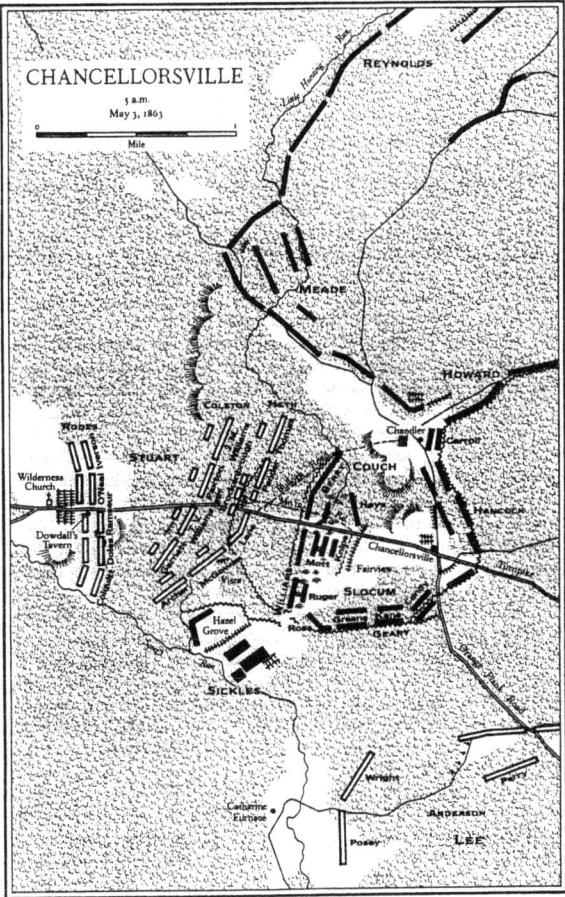

AJ.'s Company A started the battle with a strength of 72, still commanded by Captain John Mays with Colonel Folsom leading the regiment. In six days the regiment marched ten miles to Chancellorsville, then 12 miles on Jackson's flank movement, doubling back at some point to rescue the 23rd GA under attack by Sickles' division, missed Jackson's main attack on the afternoon of 2 May, rejoined Hill late that night and attacked with Heth the next day. After Lee's dispatch of McLaw and Anderson on 4 May, they (Stuart's Corps) were outnumbered three to one but held their positions against Hooker's Army. In the fighting of 3 May, Company A suffered the following casualties. Killed: Thomas A. Chambliss, Benjamin Edge, Thomas W. Williams. Wounded: Tarpley L. Curtis, William G. Gardner, John H. Phinazee, and James M. Thrash. Gardner and Thrash would return to action. Each of these two had been previously wounded at Fair Oaks and 2nd Manassas. The regiment suffered ten killed including Colonel Fielder, and nineteen others wounded.

We pick up below with the 14th writer's narrative during the latter part of the winter 1863 Fredericksburg bivouac.

"Drill, inspections, and mocked combat become a daily routine. That which drew criticism difficult to bear, centered on movements within a brigade; that is, bugle blasts were often misunderstood causing charges in the wrong directions to the maddening screams of General Thomas. Our division spent January gathering money and foodstuffs for the city of Fredericksburg whose people were destitute. There was hardly a home untouched by battle in the entire area and businesses are in ruins. As we moved our gifts up Military Road to the city, the rains were constant, and everywhere were shallow wet graves with body remains openly visible. Most were glad to get back to Camp Gregg. February 1863 is noted for the religious revival in camp. Lots of discussions on holy subjects and everybody had a different point of view. A hundred men in our regiment were allowed to go home on furlough. They gathered with men from other brigades, marched to Hamilton's Crossing and thence by rail to wherever. Sunday, March 8th comes Preacher Lyman of the 49th Georgia and he wound down about one o'clock; after which we enjoyed a meal of boiled goober peas before we marched off to picket duty on the Rappahanock River. We hear the distant whistle of Yankee locomotives coming and going. The boredom is relieved somewhat while on picket duty by trading and conversing with the Yankees across the way. Goober peas, coffee, and items taken from their dead would usually go for shoes, which we lacked more than anything else. Also they sacked anything else. Also they sacked Burnside for the tail whipping we gave them at the last battle. A general by the name of Hooker is now in charge. March 9th, 1863 gives us excellent weather but that was followed the next day with rain, snow, and sleet... sometimes one, then the other. We write letters, play cards, argue the bible, and sleep... not necessarily in that order.

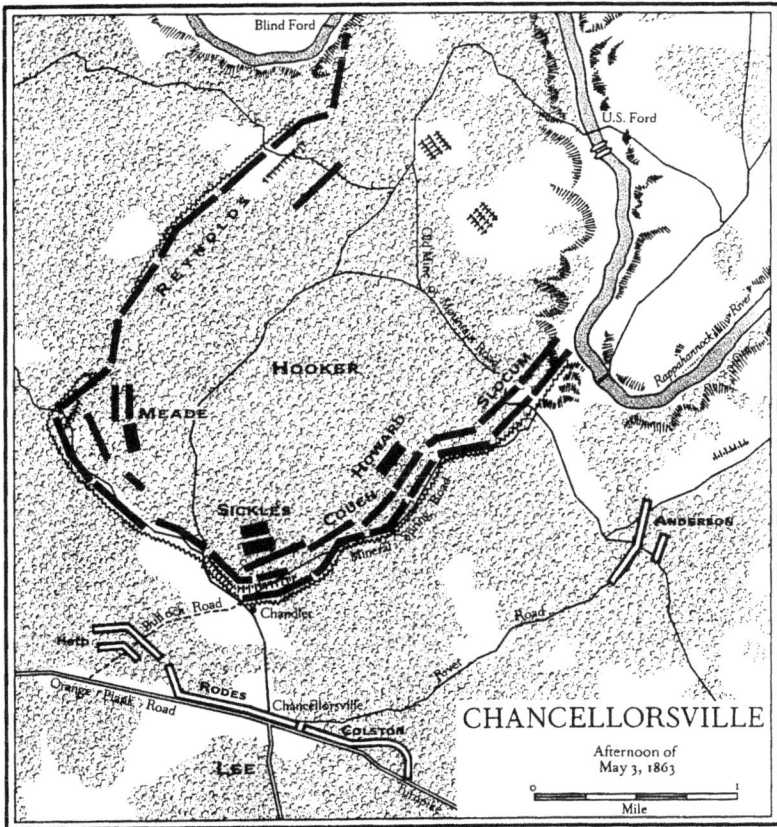

CHANCELLORSVILLE
Afternoon of
May 3, 1863

Mile

On Monday, March 10th, again cold and snowy but we hear lots of cannonading north of us. We suppose Jeb Stuart is at it again. March 12th brings the usual morning inspections and in the afternoon regimental drills. Tuesday, March 17th very heavy and constant

51

times. Wednesday, March 18th quiet everywhere. Cloudy and biting chilly in the morning and not to get better as the day progresses. But at least no cannonading as that gives everybody the willies. March 19th picket duty on the Rappahannock River. General Lee suspends all furloughs not in effect. Something about a wagon train coming from North Carolina to Richmond was the mean rumor running around but never got the whole of it. Sunday, March 22nd heard Preacher Lyman again. Inspections and drill remainder of the day until about five o'clock. Horribly windy. We are getting tired of hanging around this place. Let's fight and get this thing over with. Tuesday, March 31st. Heavy snow today and we thought it was all over with. Monday, April 6th the snows are melting fast. The 14th against the 35th in a ball game which resulted in a massive free for all fist fight. This was not a small thing. Multitudes were locked into bayonet duels but no one was seriously hurt. Summary hearings and a few court-martials came forth. Many made to dig up tree stumps. Others marked time on a pickle barrel- a rather silly thing to watch, with the barrel rolling at times. Tuesday, April 21st, 1863 comes the medical corps with vaccinations and very sore arms for all. April 25th. The Yankees are for sure stirring around with lots of cannon fire we suppose to let us know to wake up, time to fight. April 28th we start packing up, taking down tents, and tearing apart the shacks and burning them up. On the morning of the 29th we departed Camp Gregg in a cold rain, northeast winds, and plenty of mud and marched northward for twenty miles and right back into the same battle area one mile north of Hamilton's Crossing. And here we remained knee-deep in mud all day on the 30th. Early morning before light at about 4 AM we are on the march again westward stopping shortly for two hours at Salem Church, and then onward again and going into camp a short distance from Chancellorsville. A goodly part of our army was left at this point. The following morning we struck out following Stonewall Jackson into the wilderness, and to a point that only he and God knew about. With so many brigades leaving on the morning of May 2nd, ours didn't join the end of the line before eleven o'clock. Since the Jackson-Hill falling out, we being under Hill now bring up the rear and eat dust. This was a different march and no smoking or talking allowed in the most rigid way. Every man knew we were sneaking around the enemy for a flank or rear attack. We passed quietly by Catherine Furnace area and headed south. But fifteen minutes had passed and the tail end of our army was under attack making it necessary for Archer and our brigades to run back in aid. Some of the wagons and men of Best's 23rd Georgia were under attack; indeed most of them were captured. But the enemy had fled and we reversed fast. We hurried to catch up with our main army but the main attack by them was under way long before we could get there. Without us and General Archer's brigade, the enemy was still swept from the field. That night under cover of darkness, we prepared for the morning of May 3rd, ourselves making up the second line of attack, then being prepared we slept by our guns on the ground the remainder of the night obtaining whatever sleep possible, which was very little. At the crack of dawn, we rushed forward and began our work of Yankee destruction. The enemy had constructed heavy fortifications complete with breastworks but we drove them backwards and overrun their line in short order and continued our push over top of yet another second line of fortifications similar to the first. But bulging out ahead of our army had placed us in grave crossfire and we had to run backward to our former position for protection. And later that night cannon shell became so intense that we retreated even further back to our original lines. The Yankee shells set the woods afire and before our very eyes the wounded of both sides were burned alive in the most nightmarish experience that human beings could be expected to undergo. Many from both sides yelled "truce, truce" but it never happened. The morning brought a frightful scene of multiple charred bodies in their dead positions of attempts to flee the heat and flames which gave no mercy. All through the 4th we dug trenches to brace for an attack. A small place called Hazel Grove was concentrated with much of our artillery, and throughout the day it barked at the Yankee lines with fierce accuracy and this continued all day, night, and toward noon of the 5th and would have continued beyond that except for massive rains. Our two divided armies reconnected near the Chancellorsville home where the Union headquarters had been and stood watching the burning of it and we yelled at the top of our voices at the fruits of our success. Tuesday, May 6th we pulled back to a point near Orange Courthouse and then started our mud-march back to a place which all have developed a keen dislike - Hamilton's Crossing south of Fredericksburg. We hear the famed Stonewall Jackson has been wounded and taken from the field on a stretcher during the last battle. Col. Fielder was killed. Tom Chambliss and Tom Williams is dead. And the wounded in our own Company A, not to speak of the entire regiment, are too numerous to list. Tarpley Curtis was unable to see and was taken by wagon driven by George Williams, which also had Tom aboard. Monday, 11th May the camp is deeply saddened by the death of Stonewall Jackson, our commander these many years. Also Ben Edge was buried outside the hospital tent. But the war goes on and we are on picket duty at Morse's Neck. The Yankee's are gone and not even their pickets to talk or trade with. The scouts tell that the last scare sent them disorganized beyond the Rappahannock River and perhaps they might hang Hooker for allowing that last sneaker."

GETTYSBURG

With the death of Jackson after Chancellorsville, Lee had to replace this invaluable corps commander. Instead of a direct replacement, he reorganized the Army of Northern Virginia into three corps instead of two. Dependable Longstreet retained command of his corps, and Richard B. Ewell and A.P. Hill ascended to command of the other two. These two had been extremely able and aggressive division commanders under Jackson, and Lee would have preferred that they both remain at that level. Neither was yet ready for corps command, and neither would ever quite fulfill Lee's hopes.

A.P. Hill's old light division was and still is regarded as among the best in the Confederate Army. Now it was partly broken up. Archer's mixed Tennessee and Alabama brigade was moved to what would become Anderson's division of Hill's Corps. Dorsey Pender of the North Carolina brigades obtained command of Hill's old division, which now consisted of Thomas' Georgia brigade, Scales' and Lane's North Carolina brigades, and McGowan's South Carolina brigade. Harry Heth's division joined Pender and Anderson to form the three divisions of Hill's III Corps.

With his reorganized army, Lee prevailed against Davis' wish for him to remain on the defensive. In mid June the army moved north of the Potomac hoping to engage the Army of the Potomac in one last decisive battle. Here tragically Lee's beliefs in his army's invincibility finally exceeded that army's capabilities. By late June, all three corps were in Pennsylvania looking for Meade's Army. (Meade would replace Hooker on the eve of the battle at Gettysburg.)

On the morning of 1 July, Lee was with Hill's Corps, marching southeast down the Cashtown Road to Gettysburg. Heth's division led the march, followed in order by Pender and Anderson. That day Brigadier General Buford's cavalry brigade of New York and Illinois volunteers formed a thin line along Seminary Ridge, which runs for a few miles south of Gettysburg. Buford spotted Heth's division marching toward him, and though greatly outnumbered, Buford believed he occupied a good defensive position. He determined to fight on that line with the expectation of help from Reynolds' I Corps in his rear.

The three-day battle that resulted from Buford's decision to fight here remains after 140 years the biggest and bloodiest battle ever fought on the North American continent. Hundreds of thousands of pages have been written regarding it, many defending Lee's or Longstreet's decisions made there. But this is a story of the 14th GA infantry, and it did not make a large contribution to the fighting at Gettysburg after the first day. Decisions from above kept Thomas' brigade out of action. But when they fought, they won.

In the opening engagement on the morning of the first day, Heth's division advanced past Willoughby Run Creek into the fire of Buford's troopers, who held their positions for two hours waiting for Reynolds' infantry. By noon Reynolds arrived to set up a strong line running north and south across the Cashtown Rd, up to Oak Hill. With Reynolds in line, A.P. Hill accepted battle, turning this into a major engagement. Pender's division shortly joined the battle, bringing Thomas' brigade and the 14th GA into it. Colonel Folsom brought the 14th into the widening conflict this hot July day. Captain Mays still commanded Co. A's 67 soldiers. In the thickest of the fighting, Thomas' brigade deployed along both sides of the Cashtown Rd, with the 14th GA advancing along an unfinished railroad cut just north of the road.

US forces fought brilliantly at Gettysburg, but Reynolds' Corps could not match Hill's this day. Hill poured in his corps remorselessly, "and they were great fighters" (Catton, Glory Road, p. 302). Reynolds possessed certain defensive advantages, but brigade by brigade the Confederates outfought their adversaries. Thomas' brigade found itself faced off against the distinctive 1st brigade, 1st division, 1st Corps. These iron soldiers were veterans of Manassas, Antietam Creek, Fredericksburg, and Chancellorsville, but today would be their last great fight of the war. Thomas' fighters destroyed them. The 14th GA squared off against the 24th Michigan and inflicted 80% casualties.

Before the day was out Ewell's Corps had engaged Howard's XI Corps north of Gettysburg. Both Ewell and Hill were victorious, driving the enemy out of their positions, through Gettysburg, and onto Cemetery Ridge south and east of town. Reynolds himself was killed.

Major General Hancock took charge of the US line and recognized the good defensive position. Despite the day's defeat, Hancock sensed the opportunity for a victory and prepared for a general engagement. Both armies deployed in full strength as all corps elements arrived that evening. Any serious student of this conflict knows the dispositions of the two lines. We will not describe them, but will detail Hill's portion of the Confederate line.

Gettysburg

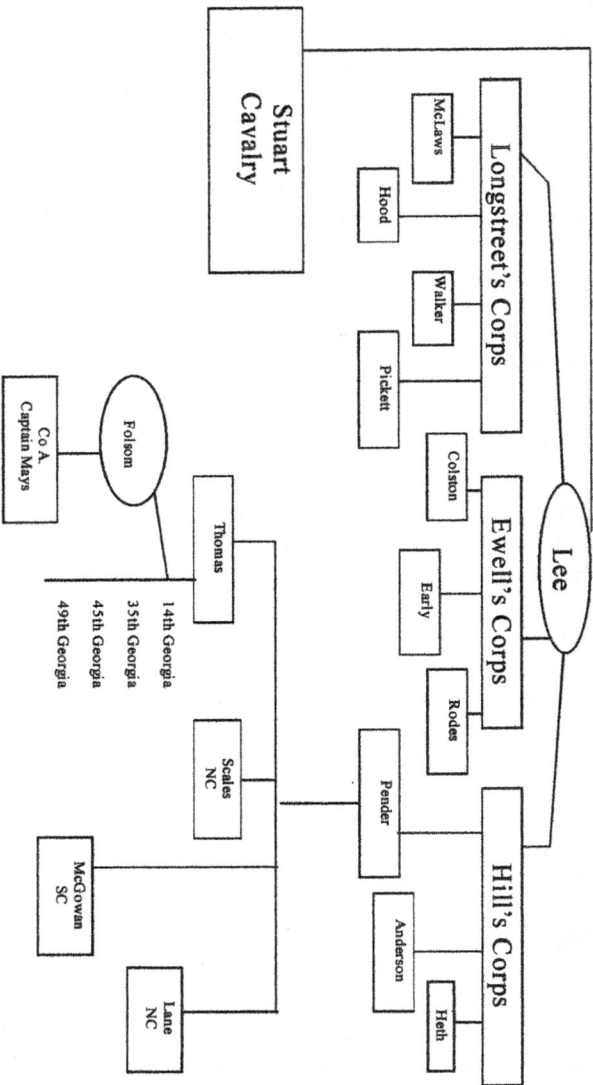

Lee

Stuart
Cavalry

Longstreet's Corps
- McLaws
- Hood
- Walker
- Pickett

Ewell's Corps
- Colston
- Early
- Rodes

Hill's Corps
- Anderson
- Heth

Pender
- Scales NC
- McGowan SC
- Lane NC

Thomas
- 14th Georgia
- 35th Georgia
- 45th Georgia
- 49th Georgia

Folsom

Co A. Captain Mays

On Thursday morning, 2 July, Lee sought Longstreet's council regarding the next move, but then would have none of it. Longstreet wanted to flank Meade's Army on the right or simply to await Meade's attack. Lee insisted on being the aggressor. He attacked both of Meade's flanks late in the day - Ewell on the left with assistance from Anderson's fresh division from Hill's Corps and Longstreet on the right with two if his divisions. For this day Pickett would stay out of the fighting. Thomas' brigade, in fact all of Pender's division, would for the most part be inactive today.

With Ewell and Longstreet on the left and right flanks, Hill's Corps occupied Lee's center in the order north to south Heth, Pender, and Anderson. From the narrative below we conclude Thomas must have been at or very near the extreme right of Pender's line. The writer refers to the Virginia, Alabama, and Mississippi units to his near right. These are three of Anderson's brigades of Hill's Corps. The 5th and 8th Florida are also part of that division.

A.J.'s Company A must have had an excellent view of the valley between Seminary and Cemetery Ridges, and thus a good view of much of the Peach Orchard and wheatfield where Longstreet hit Sickles' division. US forces fought well this day, and both flank attacks failed to capture the ends of Meade's line. Both sides suffered very heavy casualties. Pender's division was idle, but still they sustained casualties from US artillery. General Pender was mortally wounded on the afternoon of this day.

On the morning of 3 July, Longstreet again urged Lee to await Meade's attack or to flank him on the right to draw him out of his fortified positions. Again Lee would have none of it. He ordered an assault on Meade's center across the mile-wide open valley and up the gentle slope of Cemetery Ridge. The attack would be led by General Pickett's fresh division with help from two of Hill's scratch divisions led today by Trimble and Pettigrew. Longstreet protested that "no 15,000 men who ever lived could make that attack successfully," but the assault went forward.

The Confederate assault of 3 July at Gettysburg has become glorified as Pickett's Charge, but in fact Hill contributed more men to it. Pickett's three Virginia brigades spearheaded the charge, but in it also were Heth's four brigades led today by General Pettigrew and two of Pender's brigades led today by General Trimble.

The artillery barrage opened at 1 PM from the Confederate Army. It was the biggest this army had yet or would ever sustain, lasting about 90 minutes, concentrating on Hancock's Corps in Meade's center. Shortly after 2:30 the Confederate infantry assembled for the attack. The writer below tells of the "South Carolina regiments to our left" (McGowan's brigade of Pender's division) and of the 47th and other Virginia regiments to our right commanded by a Colonel Mayo"

(Walker's brigade of Heth's division) preparing for the charge. Thomas' brigade again was mercifully held in reserve to repel a counterattack.

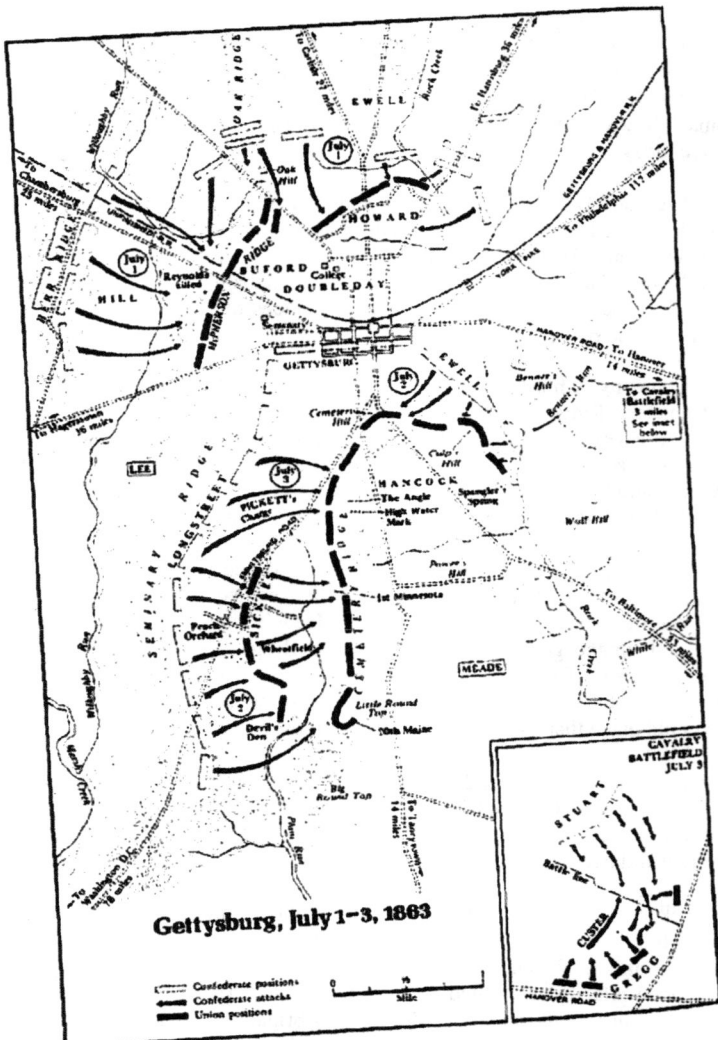

Gettysburg, July 1-3, 1863

The infantry divisions assembled from northeast, facing Cemetery Hill, to southwest facing the beginning of Plum Run, in the order Trimble, Pettigrew, Pickett - forty-seven regiments, nine brigades, two and a half divisions, more than one fourth of Lee's Army charged up Cemetery Ridge hoping today's action would end the war. Never again in any war would such a massive body of men charge an enemy position in the old style. The United States Army demonstrated to General Lee and to the rest of the world that this kind of warfare was obsolete.

At 2:30, when the Confederate artillery ceased fire, Lt. General Longstreet, who was opposed to this assault with all his heart, could not give the order to advance. Major General Pickett had to prompt him with "General, shall I advance?" Longstreet, in overwhelming sadness could only nod. Bruce Catton, probably the premier biographer of the Army of the Potomac, describes the day's fighting in moving detail in the last chapter of his book Glory Road. Interested readers should not pass up this account. Quoting from his description of Pickett's charge:

"The smoke lifted like a rising curtain, and all the great amphitheater lay open at last, and the Yankee soldiers could look west all the way up to the belt of trees on Seminary Ridge. They were old soldiers and had been in many battles, but what they saw then took their breath away, and whether they had ten minutes of seventy-five years to live, they remembered it until they died. There it was, for the last time in this war, perhaps for the last time ever, the grand pageantry of war in the old style. Lee was putting fifteen thousand men into this column - George Pickett was riding into storybook immortality with his division of Virginians, coming out of the woods to march across a mile wide valley to the heights where the Yankees were waiting with shotted guns."

A.J. and the rest of the 14th GA infantry watched, perhaps North America's most dramatic hour, from the heights of Seminary Ridge. Pettigrew's and Trimble's divisions were the first to melt away. They evaporated from the unmerciful artillery fire. Pickett's Virginians did not quit. They were engulfed in enfilading artillery and rifle fire from the front and right. Most were casualties or became prisoner. The division did not ever again fight as a unit. The Confederates suffered a defeat from which they could not recover.

Meade did not counter Lee's unsuccessful assault. Lee's Army escaped in the next several days, crossing into Virginia on 13 July. In the three days at Gettysburg the Confederates lost the initiative forever. In A.J.'s Co. A, Corporal Absalom Baldwin and Pvt. John Dumas were killed. Pvts. James Dewberry and Asberry Hawthorne were wounded and captured. James Dewberry is listed as captured on 5 July, thus we must conclude he was left by the army to be captured in hospital. Finally in this three-day battle we tally the 14th GA casualties. Fifteen were wounded, thirteen killed, and twenty-seven were captured (seven with wounds). The 14th writer below describes the Gettysburg engagement beginning almost a month before.

"Monday, June 8th, 1863, a colorful parade assembly with citations pinned on our brigade and regimental flags. General Thomas is given special commendations, which we feel good about and our wounded General Ambrose Hill receives certain awards as well and both are heroes in our eyes. The Richmond newspapers seem to agree on this. But while these events and extra cannonading from our side increased, rumors are wild in camp about our army pulling out and heading westward and the space between our troops and units are being spread evermore widely as the pull out continues day after day. Also posted for reading is that the "light division" under General Hill no longer exists and instead the Army or Northern Virginia is now organized into three parts with each called a corps. We will be the Third Corps. By June 13th the Yankees begin to thin out also with much fewer pickets and in some areas none. And on the morning of June 14th we also left the area and headed west toward Chancellorsville. Our whole army had faded westward and we obviously were last out. We past through the last battlefield area with little conversation. The burnt out woods, half buried corpses, rotting horseflesh, half gone forests and other evidence of recent war were everywhere to be seen. So it was good to pass quickly on through the area. And afterward, the troops seem to gain stability and morale. Regimental and brigade flags were unfurled. Slow, fast, and sometimes even fancy drumbeats sounded and songs were sung. The 35th Georgia had the best harmonizers and we enjoyed listening to them sing but grossly disliked them as a group and dubbed them as the "braggarts of the brigade". The 14th and 45th often intermingled mainly because of blood kin in both. By evening of June 17th we were marching through Culpepper. The inhabitants were haggard and famine marked their faces and the difference between last year and today was the talk of the company. By early morning of the 19th we started into the Blue Ridge Mountain range by way of Chester's

Gap and near noon on the 20th we were at Front Royal and we did not linger but continued two miles north to the Shenandoah River. A boat bridge across had been built and men and wagons were crossing but not fast enough and a pileup of thousands were in fields and along the banks. Millions of bats from mountain caves were everywhere to be seen darting and diving after men's caps were thrown into the air. And soon thousands were engaged in the slaughter of bats with sticks as they followed hats to the ground and this went for hours. By the 22nd of June 1863 we went past Berryville, and the 23rd was at Shepherdstown and late that evening crossed the Potomac River, past through Sharpsburg, Maryland on the 24th listening to many stories from the previous year. Thomas' brigade had missed this battle last year since we were at the time transacting business at Harper's Ferry. Through heavy rains we marched on reaching Hagerstown, Maryland and past into the great state of Pennsylvania on the 26th of June 1863. Certain it is that we shall run into the Yankee Army somewhere up here, and equally certain it is that we shall beat their tails. On the 27th we past Chambersburg and turned eastward and encamped near a small community called Fayetteville. Remaining here on the 28th and 29th, we moved just beyond Cashtown on the 30th of June 1863. On July first we were up early at 5 AM and dressed for march in a slow drizzle of rain and we fell in to go and here we stood while brigade after brigade left. Finally, with half the morning gone, we left also a full hour behind the rest. Since grease cans were past around last night and a full ration of whiskey this morning, then we suppose the Yankee army must be close by. But eastward we went down the Chambersburg Pike and soon heard the boom of cannon at a distance and upon reaching a small creek called Willoughby Run began to observe stragglers from some of the units that had passed before us. Many wounded being attended to and laying along the creek bed. We begin to deploy to the left and to the right with the 14th regiment walking forward on the left side of the pike near a new railroad bank. Before finishing our deployment the charge bugle sounded and off we run splashing across the creek and up the ravine amid a terrible spray of grape and musket minnie. The Yankee famed Iron Brigade was caught in the stampede and few were able to escape back into the City of Gettysburg, Pennsylvania. And we charged past many of our own exhausted brigades, and many unwounded were pressed ahead of us into the doing of their duty. And the stubborn enemy began to waiver and finally break and routed down the ridge with hundreds of the slow runners being captured and from the heights we could see some of our own army entering the city. But we were bugled southward onto

Seminary Ridge, which had just been cleared of the enemy and here we, part of Thomas' brigade and sister brigades gather for further direction from General Pender. None came and until we slept, across the way came forth sure sounds of preparations by the enemy of breastworks, ditches, and the marches of multitudes gathering to do battle. Creaks of the wheels coupled with grunts of horses define without doubt the placement of cannon. July 2nd, 1863. Thursday. Up early and deployed on the eastside of Seminary Ridge and waiting for the bugle to attack. And we waited. The morning past quickly with little and the summer heat was becoming extreme. Our deployments could easily be seen by the enemy, and the shells were increasing by the hour. As General Pender rode along our waiting lines, one of the incoming shells exploded nearby seriously wounding him and two other staff officers riding with him and they were taken from the field by stretchers-bearers. The wait continued until well after four o'clock at which time to our extreme right our army's cannon opened upon the enemy even as an extreme clap of thunder and as the evening progressed the Alabama, Virginia, and Mississippi outfits located just to our right charged down the ravine into battle and disappeared into the thick smoke collecting. We stood up and waited for our own bugles to blow. But the signal never came and near dark many of us ran down the ravine to help the returning wounded of the 5th and 8th Florida Regiments back up the hill and the mass numbers of the wounded were shocking to behold among General Wilcox's Alabama regiments. July 3rd, 1863. Was up before daylight this Friday morning fully expecting to share in whatever was to come. A number of South Carolina regiments to our left and the 47th Virginia Regiment to our right commanded by a Colonel Mayo who appeared to be over the other Virginia regiments nearby. As was the case yesterday we waited through out the morning. Many sewed their names into their shirts, a depressing thing to watch. But many saw this battle as Fredericksburg in reverse. The Yankees had the heights instead of us and is next to impossible to capture. Our failure to do so yesterday failed to add hope to this morning. A spectacle heretofore unknown among us were the multiple prayer circles openly engaged in by officers and ranks. At about five minutes after one o'clock the artillery to our rear and to our right opened upon the enemy heights across the way and continued for at least two hours. The very trees seem to dance on top of the ground and the whole of Seminary Ridge whereon we stood rocked and reeled as though hell itself was attempting to break free. Shortly after three o'clock the bugles of our army began to sound forward the charge and everyone to our right went forward but we and everyone to the left of us did not. And Colonel Folsom and staff came galloping by stating we would be held in reserve and to ready for a counter-attack if our army did not fare well. Our army did not fare well and thousands were killed and wounded. The sight of their return, at least those spared, was a nightmare to behold and we could not leave our defenses to help as done last night but waited for the counter-offensive which never came. July 4th, 1863. Saturday. Periodic shells though out the night made sleep most difficult. Waiting for enemy attacks which never happened. Very cloudy and early afternoon brought forth a drizzle and by nightfall, we formed in the muddy roads and headed south and march all night. No smoking or torches of any kind. Mud, muck, and mire at times up to our knees and the whole moving disorganized at snails pace- but still in the direction of dear ole Virginia and safety. We retreated on through Fairfield reaching them by four o'clock the following day. The villages and farms are no longer immune from their stocks and foodstuffs. We take as we go and how the locals squeal. July 7, 1863. On the heights between Hagarstown and Williamsport digging trenches and waiting for Meade's Yankees half of us digging, the other half sleeping in the mud. As we prepared for the expected Yankee attack, our army's engineers were building a pontoon bridge across the Potomac River under trying circumstances without which escape would be impossible. But finally it was completed by the 13th of July and our men and equipment went over at a place called Falling Water. The South Carolina unit next to us on Seminary Ridge was attacked just before it passed over the river by Yankee cavalry who seriously wounded General Pettigrew. Of the attacking Yankee force of seventy-five, all were killed of the 6th Michigan cavalry save six and they were brought over the pontoon bridge to join the others guarded by the 45th. And we watched as the pontoons were cut on our side and shot away by cannon on the far shore and the thankful cheers of thousands as the many boats were carried by the angry rain swollen current swiftly down stream. We then marched twenty miles and went into camp just west of Bunker Hill, Virginia at a place called Mill Creek. July 19th 1863. Word comes to us that General Pettigrew died here at Bunker Hill and our own General Dorsey Pender died yesterday at the Staunton, Virginia hospital. Again we broke camp and marched to Chester Gap and continued across the Blue Ridge Mountains and into Culpepper. A lot of our wounded were housed in the hospital here and we took time to visit them."

Lee's defeated and depleted army limped back into Virginia having suffered a devastating 20-30% casualties at Gettysburg. In the 14ᵗʰ GA, A.J. had to leave his wounded brother James to capture. Lee's Army retreated through Virginia traveling east of the Blue Ridge Mountains badly needing to avoid contact with Meade's Army. Meade followed Lee south, but kept his army west of the mountains. For the rest of 1863 there were no major engagements, granting Lee the respite his army needed. By 1 August the 14ᵗʰ GA had obtained yet another (its third) division commander. Major General Wilcox was moved from Longstreet's Corp to obtain command of Pender's division of A.P. Hill's Corps. Wilcox would keep the division for the rest of the war.

During the hiatus on the Virginia front, fighting elevated to an accelerated pace in the West. On 9 September, Rosecrans moved his army south toward Georgia. Longstreet's Corps was quickly transferred from Lee's command to Bragg's to help meet this threat. Longstreet's men joined the field on 19-20 September to help Bragg drive Rosecrans out of Georgia. General U.S. Grant attained supreme command in the West, and the November battles of Lookout Mountain and Missionary Ridge became important US victories. Longstreet remained with Bragg until near the end of 1863, at which time his corps was dispatched as an independent command to operate in North Carolina and Tennessee. This dependable corps finally rejoined Lee in May 1864 in the midst of the Battle of the Wilderness.

On the Virginia front on 14 October 1863, A.P. Hill, acting independently, sent two North Carolina brigades of Wilcox's division into a trap at Bristoe Station, near Manassas. The division took 2,000 casualties that day, with nothing accomplished. Very little is written of this engagement, and very little was said in Lee's Army about it. However from here on till the war's end, Lee lost and never regained confidence in Hill as a corps commander. Lee would never again allow Hill freedom on the battlefield. This would prove costly in May 1864 with an important lost opportunity at the North Anna River.

The eye-witness accounts continue.

"We learn that General Cadmus Wilcox is now our divisional commander. On Monday, August 3ʳᵈ, 1863 the whole of Third Corps is on the move toward Orange Courthouse, a days march southward perhaps twenty miles and while they are in this process, our brigade is shifting to the overpass at the Rapidan River for picket duty. But the following day, we were relieved for reasons unknown and marched back to a place among our regular army who had now established themselves in a cornfield a mile outside of Orange Courthouse. This is a massive encampment with soldiers setting up in every direction the eyes look. The former wounded are returning and new recruits added. Flour, bacon, potatoes, and other items are coming in great abundance. Clothing and shoes are also being provided. Apples and blackberries are also plentiful. August 26th. A deserter was tied to a pole and shot amid a lot of loud drum beating. September 21st corps grand review with General Lee present. A lot of pretty ladies were present from distant places. We render the air with three cheers in honor of General Lee to demonstrate our continued support and indeed it was sincere and heartfelt as we felt his need. And at first a few, and then many, and then most, stood forth and raised his right arm to the square and yelled "to the death" and this many times. As we marched past the reviewing stand, we could see he was well pleased and the camp's critics were no longer to be found for fear of the great majority. Shooting deserters begins to be the talk of the camp. General Lane of the North Carolina outfits has shot at least ten during this month alone; ours only two. Desertions are very few and those AWOL are returning by the multitudes. The manpower strength of our brigade has more than doubled while here at Orange. Another extremely noticeable change is religious revivals – they are everywhere and the whole army is alive with it. Forty-five, including Colonel Folsom, in our 14th regiment were baptized on the 21st of September 1863 on the banks of the Rapidan in plain sight of Yankee pickets. We notice a part of Longstreet's command are no longer in their place; they indeed have slowly been pulling out for the past two weeks but now have become the talk of the camp. Are we leaving also and go where they went? Tuesday, September 22nd, picket duty on the Rapidan. Thursday, September 24th. Back in our Orange position enjoying the boredom of camp life. Thursday, October 1 Walker's Ford on the ole Rapidan River doing the usual picket duty trading and talking with Yankee pickets. They tell us of an overwhelming defeat of the Union Army out west by General Longstreet. If one wants to know anything about our army, one need only ask a Yankee picket. Rumors are flying that our whole army was heading west to Tennessee and beyond. October 8th at Burnet's Ford and picket duty until nine o'clock that night. October 9th, 1863. Up before daylight with yells and screams everywhere to be heard and the whole army is on the move. October 10th, marched through Madison, Virginia and afterward broke into a double time toward Culpeper Courthouse, arriving on the 11th. The Yankees had pulled out in a hurry leaving a small amount of equipment behind. We are totally exhausted after running clean around

Cedar Mountain hoping to capture a goodly part of the Yankee army, but that came to naught and a severe disappointment to us all but we continued hot pursuit toward Warrenton, Virginia entering it on the afternoon of October 13th. That night a big red glow on the skyline east of us indicated mass Yankee burnings as they retreated. Wednesday, October 14th leaving in the early morning hours, we run awhile and walk awhile hoping to catch up with the retreating northern armies but only finding burning camp fires but no Yankee army. Heading down the Auburn Mills Road, it is obvious the Yankees are running scared as knapsacks, canteens, overcoats, and foods litter the road side. At last we arrived on the heights overlooking Broad Run and Bristoe Station areas to see multiple thousands of the enemy covering the plains across the creek. Our cannon opened sending them into panic in every direction and down the road went several North Carolina regiments and poured across the plains aligning themselves and running forward at the same time. Our brigade watched from the heights as the Yankee trap snapped shut. The enemy's thousands hiding behind the Bristoe Railroad embankment and the distant Yankee artillery killed and captured a goodly portion of North Carolina's finest right before our eyes. The area had been pinpointed for artillery before our arrival because the explosions all happened at exactly the same time. It was obvious to us all that our General Hill should have recon the area with cavalry before rushing troops in. The enemy that we had pursued so hard and fast simply pulled out of the area with us standing on the heights watching as no further effort or attack on our part took place. And as the Generals and staff came for a closer look at the carnage, no one spoke or waved for we were mad at them. October 15th, in a hard rain, we ventured down and helped gather the wounded and bury the dead, both of which numbered at least two thousand. October 16th. We are on the march in hard rains pursuing the Yankee army into the Bull Run area and waited receiving unaimed shells to slow pursuit. But Meade's Army kept going apparently wanting no part of a third Bull Run. Our cannons were mired in mud and the chase was over but not the war and we went to work tearing up the Orange and Alexandria Railroad tracks between Bristoe Station and the Rappahannock Bridge which itself had been blown up by the Yankee army. But we did more by burning up each crosstie and afterward went back across the river, dug in and waited. Monday, October 26th. Went to picket duty on the Rapidan and relieved the 14th South Carolina. Shot at some Yankee cavalry watering their horses. One unhorsed, bowed gracefully, returned to saddle, and slowly left amid some limited hand claps from our side. Their pickets inform us that General Hill was under arrest for the Bristoe Station debacle and it became the talk of the camp. But General Thomas assured the rumor to be false and that General Hill was very much in command and Lee assured that nothing further would be said or done. So that night we reassured our Yankee friends they would yet face Hill again and they acted happy, but don't think they were. So things pretty much continued until November 8th when a big alert is sounded and word comes the Yankee army is on the move. President Jefferson Davis came for review on November 25th and we endured a long speech in a cold rain. The following day we left the Clark's Mountain area, and on the following 27th, positioned ourselves in a line of battle across the Orange Turnpike which ran almost side by side with the Orange Plank Road; and the whole of our little army of "light division" faced Mine Run. November 30th night. Through most of the cold night we massed in the woods south of Orange Plank Road to flank attack the enemy; this done, we went forward in a rush the morning of December 1st to find no enemy whatever. A severe disappointment and genuine remorse over this pullout as felt we could pen the Yankee army against the Mine Run for an artillery slaughter from which he wouldn't likely survive. So God was good to the Yankees and we marched back to the area of Clark's Mountain close in on the south side and went into camp. On Tuesday, December 16, 1863, we left the main Third Corps army at Clark's Mountain and marched to Orange Courthouse and boarded train cars to Staunton, Virginia, changing only at Gordonville. From there we marched to Buffalo Gap by foot and encamped. Ice was everywhere to be seen with tree limbs bowed to the ground. On Saturday, December 19th returned to Staunton, Virginia and rode the train cars to Milborough and camped near the train tracks. The winds and temperature rendered matters unbearably cold. Nearby was an old man's wooded picket fence, which our regiment proceeded to take down all around the entire home; then to pile same up, including the gate, and burn for warmth. That not being enough the troops fanned out over the whole village pulling down fences which added fuel to a bonfire no doubt observed by the lurking enemy on the distant mountain tops. But it also attracted the attention of General Thomas who rode into camp so fast and set forth a dressing down that was difficult to live down for months. Over seventy dollars was extracted from all, even those who had no part, and turned over to the elderly gentleman. That was an expensive fire but at least we had a warm night with a degree of sleep. On December 24th, we marched around a nearby mountain and camped near New Market and was visited by two of the three young ladies that had followed us to

Fredericksburg last year. They rode about camp on horseback shaking hands and laughing loudly but remained in saddle and left in two hours time not to be seen again. We suppose their hometown connections was the reason for the businesslike approach. On Christmas day, the people of New Market treated us with free pies and other goodies; indeed, multitudes of table were spread to overflow and lavishly set forth in great abundance. It was a royal sacrifice on their part, especially considering wartime conditions. The unusual kindness was ever a part of our conversation. On December 29, 1863, a clear but very cold day. We marched through Mount Jackson and camped in our favorite spot, which we had occupied in November 1861. December 30th we marched beyond Woodstock and encamped and the following morning continued our march in very cold rain to Strasburg, Virginia. December 31st watched two soldiers of the "Louisiana Tigers" get tied to stakes and shot amid the usual roll of drums. January 3rd, 1864 made an arc march through Hardy and Grant Counties to a point just south of Strasburg called Fisher's Hill and camped overnight, then by rail back to Mount Jackson, then by foot back to Staunton arriving January 12th. A tremendous number of our men are now developing rheumatism in their backs and knees. Back rubbings to each other are common place in our camp now with hot moss and lime dust. On January 22nd, we marched to Harrisonburg in Rockingham County and into winter quarters, which indeed was long overdue. Written passes are plentiful and this is the greatest area for resting and rousing in the entire State. Companies took turns as the provost guard within the city and things went fairly orderly throughout our stay here. But to our surprise we remained here until March 1st, 1864 and departed in the cold rain and marched 80 miles back to our regular command at Orange Courthouse of Thomas' brigade, Wilcox's division, and General A.P. Hill's Corps and thence back to the daily grind of regimental and brigade training."

WILDERNESS

Grant and Meade opened the spring 1864 campaign by moving across the Rapidan in early May. US forces in Virginia were near 120,000 against Lee's two corps of about 60,000. Meade's Army crossed the Rapidan at Germana Ford on 5 May hoping for battle south of the Wilderness area. Lee quickly countered with his two corps to force battle in the thick Wilderness area where Meade's superior numbers and superior artillery would count for less.

With Longstreet's Corps still south near Richmond, having not yet rejoined Lee after his winter campaign in Tennessee, Lee marched Ewell's Corps east on the Orange Turnpike and A.P. Hill's Corps east on the Orange Plank Road on the morning of 5 May. Ewell made first contact with Meade's Army about four miles west of Chancellorsville, but had orders to lay back and not to bring on a general engagement. Later that morning Hill's Corps made contact at the Brock Road-Orange Plank Road intersection.

Hill's Corps advanced that morning with Heth's division in the lead as at Gettysburg. Hill hoped to cut the Brock Road south, but Hancock's Corps of Meade's Army arrived first. Heth immediately attacked to gain the crossroad, and the general engagement began. Both of Lee's corps became engaged in heavy fighting separated by about three miles of dense wilderness. Heth's division pushed onward down the Orange Plank Road, getting within 50 yards of the Brock Road intersection. Wilcox's division deployed north of the Orange Plank Road in support of Heth and filling the center between Hill and Ewell along what is today Ewell-Hill Drive. Thomas' brigade occupied the northern-most portion of Wilcox's line, establishing contact with Ewell's right just northeast of the Tapp Farm. But a flanking movement around Heth's right soon created an emergency along Hill's entire front. Hill personally pulled Thomas' brigade out of the center and hustled the four regiments south toward the Plank Road to counter the US movement. Kirkland's brigade of Heth's division was in serious trouble just north of the road as Hancock poured in division after division. Hill had pulled Thomas out of the center at just the right moment to avert disaster at this point. Quoting from Dowdey in Lee's Last Campaign:

> "There Kirkland's flank was engulfed by swarms of the enemy, some working around to the rear....The density of the saplings and the under brush in that area prevented the loosely grouped Federal units from forming a perpendicular line for enfilade fire on Heth's flank, and for the moment they did not seem to recognize their advantage. In that moment of grace, Thomas' four Georgia regiments crashed their way to Kirkland's rescue...The enemy troops who had been pushing towards Heth's rear turned on Thomas' fresh regiments. Disorganized, the panting men of both sides merged in a violent, personal, formless action. Thomas' men were fighting at right angles to one another and even back to back. When even officers, drawing back from the mobs, could not see twenty yards in any direction, such military objectives as flanks ceased to be a factor. The single absorbing purpose of Hill's men, from privates to Wilcox, was to refuse to break backward."

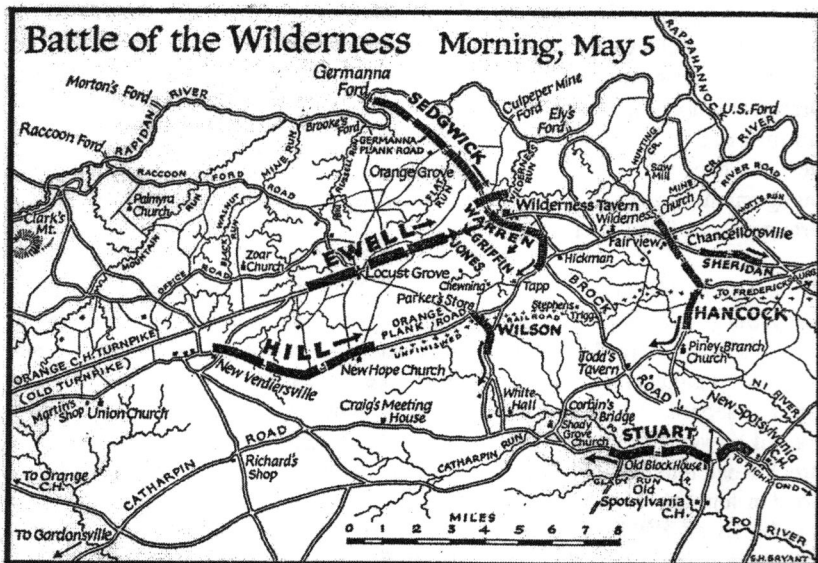

Battle of the Wilderness Morning, May 5

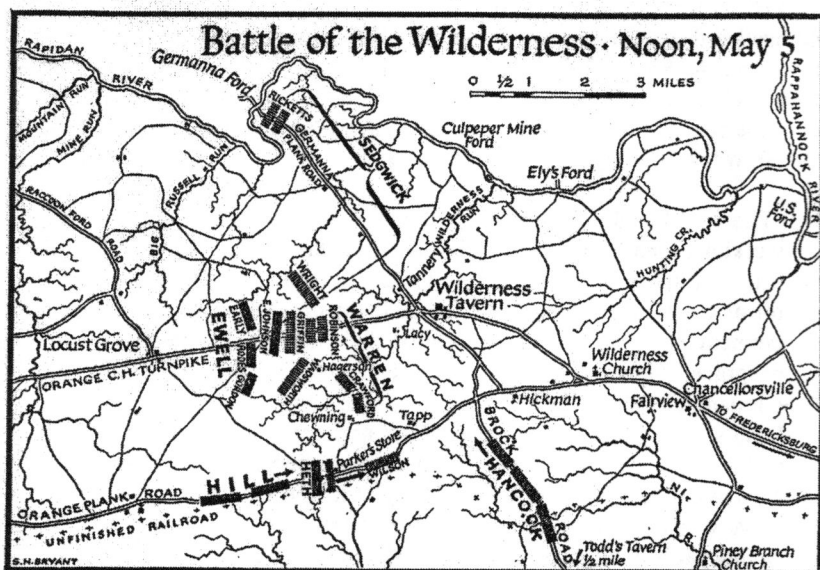

Battle of the Wilderness · Noon, May 5

70

Confused fighting continued from mid afternoon until darkness. Hill's front was outnumbered two to one, and in assessing Hill's chances to hold, Colonel Venable of Lee's staff expressed the sentiments of every soldier on the field when he muttered "if night would only come." When night did come, Hill rested with pride in his corps' performance. Again quoting from Dowdey:

> "Fought into exhaustion, with their lines split into broken fragment without form or order, his (Hill's) fourteen thousand had contained more than twice their number...Not one enemy regiment fought poorly, no alignments had been faulty and no enemy flanks had hung in the air. The Third Corps' divisions had stood up to the best there was, and high-strung Hill's heart overflowed with pride for every man in his corps."

Hill, like Grant, was a soldier's general, and on this night perceived his corps needed rest more than anything else. He disregarded pleas from both Heth and Wilcox to straighten his front, which had become mixed with US forces all up and down the line. As the quotations below demonstrate, the 14th GA was completely entangled with the 96th Pennsylvania. Hill has taken severe criticism for not taking charge and bringing order to his lines that night. He expected Longstreet at any time to come relieve his corps. So Lee had ordered, and had communicated to Hill. By midnight Lee knew Longstreet could not arrive before dawn, but did not inform Hill. Lee knew Longstreet would be late, but did not know the condition of Hill's line. Hill knew the condition of his line, but was not aware of Longstreet's delay. The dawn US attack crushed Hill's ragged line.

At dawn on May 6 the Federals launched a massive assault astride the Orange Plank Road against the two divisions of A. P. Hill's Corps that included the 14th Georgia. The 14th maintained its position, "fighting with the resolution of despair" for a short time, until the Federals got around the regiment's right flank and nearly surrounded it. One man in the 14th remembered the enemy advancing in three columns and "cross firing on our brigade . . . from the front, right flank, and rear." The Georgians had almost exhausted their ammunition "when our right flank was nearly all captured and killed and we were ordered to retire." When the order to retreat came, Colonel Folsom attempted to take his regiment out in order. Before he could do so a ball struck him in the chest, inflicting a mortal wound.

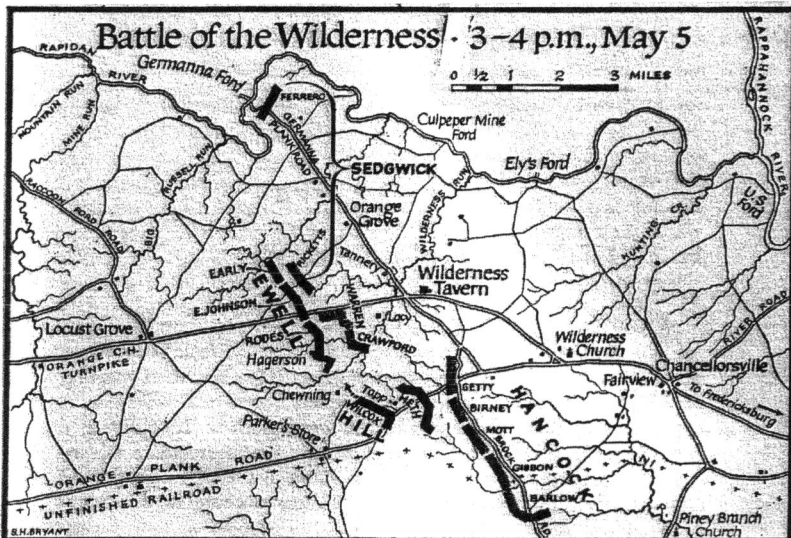

Battle of the Wilderness · 3–4 p.m., May 5

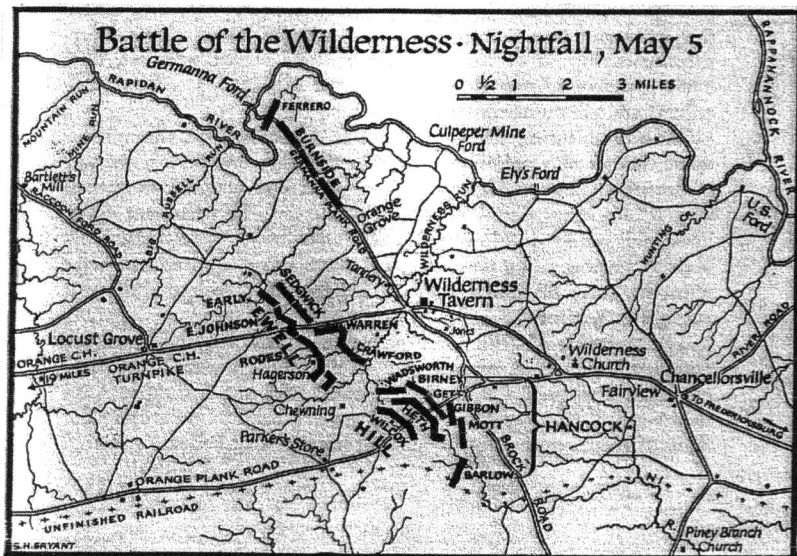

Battle of the Wilderness · Nightfall, May 5

Hill's center and right retreated about 1,000 yards in about one hour of post-dawn fighting. If not for the close firing of Hill's corps artillery from Colonel William Poague and for the timely arrival of Longstreet's Corps, who could guess the consequences to Lee's Army that morning? At about 7AM the 14th GA and all of Wilcox's division as well as Heth's had been driven back to near Tapp's Farm. At that point, we quote again from Lee's Last Campaign:

> "When Powell Hill saw his men being driven and knew that Longstreet's troops could not get up in time, he directed Poague to load his guns with antipersonal ammunition and to open up along the road as soon as he could clear the heads of their own retreating infantry. Firing obliquely at point blank range, Poague shaved the heads of his own infantrymen so narrowly that probably some of them were struck. But where the Federal troops were bunched along the road, his bursting cannister was deadlier than the fire of a full brigade."

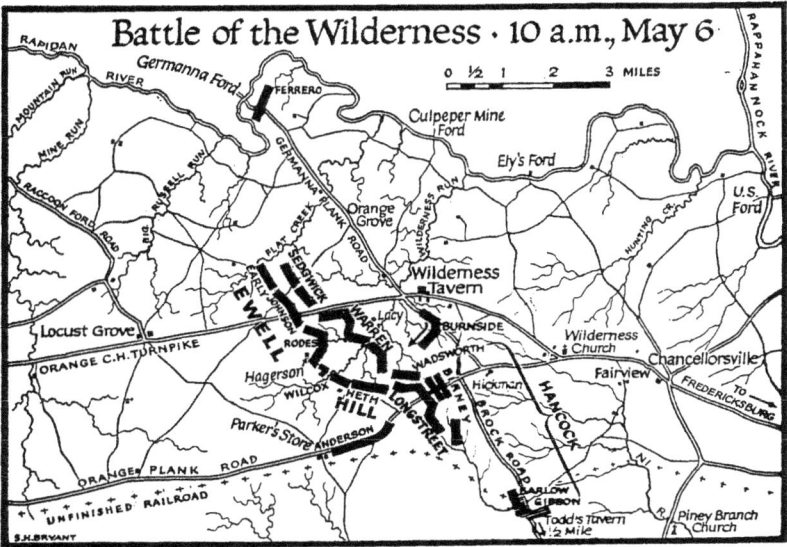

Battle of the Wilderness · 10 a.m., May 6

RAPIDAN
RAPPAHANNOCK RIVER
Germanna Ford
MOUNTAIN RUN
MINE RUN
RIVER
FERRERO
0 ½ 1 2 3 MILES
Culpeper Mine Ford
Ely's Ford
RACCOON FORD ROAD
RUSSELL RUN
GERMANNA PLANK ROAD
FLAT CREEK RUN
WILDERNESS RUN
HUNTING RUN
U.S. Ford
Orange Grove
Wilderness Tavern
SEDGWICK
Locust Grove
EWELL
ORANGE C.H. TURNPIKE
RODES
WARREN
WADSWORTH
Lacy
BURNSIDE
Wilderness Church
Chancellorsville
TO FREDERICKSBURG
Hagerson
WILCOX
HETH
HILL
LONGSTREET
Hickman
Fairview
HANCOCK
Parker's Store
ANDERSON
ORANGE PLANK ROAD
BROCK ROAD
UNFINISHED RAILROAD
BARLOW
GIBBON
Todd's Tavern ½ Mile
Piney Branch Church
S.H. BRYANT

73

Simultaneous with Poague's deadly fire, Longstreet's lead regiments hit the field after an all night march and with no breakfast. To Lee's and Hill's great relief, Longstreet's Corps collided with the US assault and completely turned the tide. From then on Longstreet owned the initiative. Lee yielded the Plank Road portion of the field to Longstreet, who was at his shining best this day. By 10AM Longstreet had halted the US advance and had saved Lee's extreme right. Hill had reformed his corps and had deployed Wilcox and Heth into the gap connecting Ewell to the Plank Road portion of the battlefield. Hill's division filled this gap just in time to contain an 11AM attack by Burnside's fresh corps. With his front fairly stable, Longstreet conceived a flanking attack on the US left, which appeared to succeed as well, though on a much smaller scale, as Jackson's flank attack of almost exactly one year earlier. As in Jackson's flank assault, Longstreet was mistakenly shot from his horse by his own men in the early afternoon. But for Longstreet's wounding and Ewells' failure to attack in more than brigade strength on his front, many Confederate historians have predicted a great victory for Lee's Army on this day.

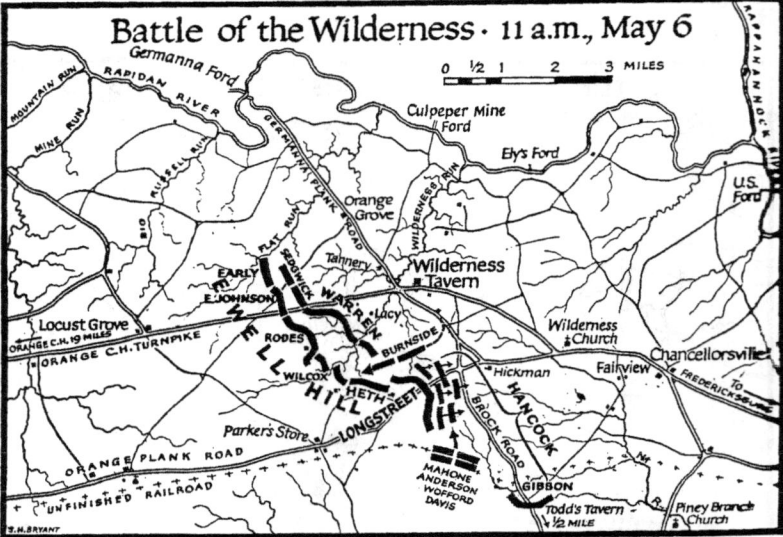

Battle of the Wilderness · 11 a.m., May 6

A.J.'s Company A started the Wilderness campaign with a company strength of 64. Captain Mays led the company, and Colonel Folsom commanded the regiment. The writer below makes no reference to the 5 May fighting near the Brock Road in which we know Thomas' brigade shared an important part, but the disorder of the lines in the night is confirmed. In the dawn assault of 6 May and in the subsequent fighting against Burnside's Corps later in the day, the company took 14% casualties. Wounded were Captain Mays, Sergeant Joseph Davis, and Privates Samual Ingram, Andrew Moran, James Riddle, James Dewberry, and Enoch Rogers. Captured were Privates Henry Jones, Alexander Kelly, and John Christian. Overall the regiment took more than 10% casualties including ten killed, 37 wounded, and 29 captured. Among the mortally wounded was Colonel Folsom, who died of his wounds on 24 May. Most of these casualties occurred on 6 May, but many occurred on 5 May, thus placing the regiment in the 5 May fighting.

Colonel Folsom was one of many casualties sustained by the 14th Georgia on the morning of May 6 as the men ran through the dense woods to escape the advancing Federals. Private James W. Dewberry was shot in the right leg. Fortunately he escaped capture and made it to a field hospital. After enduring a lengthy ambulance ride, Dewberry entered the Confederate General Hospital in Charlottesville, Virginia. Dewberry remained in the Charlottesville Hospital until May 29, when he received a furlough for sixty days starting from May 27. During this time, the wounded soldier undoubtedly went home to Monroe County to recover with his family. By June 30, 1864, James Dewberry had rejoined his brother and comrades in the 14th.

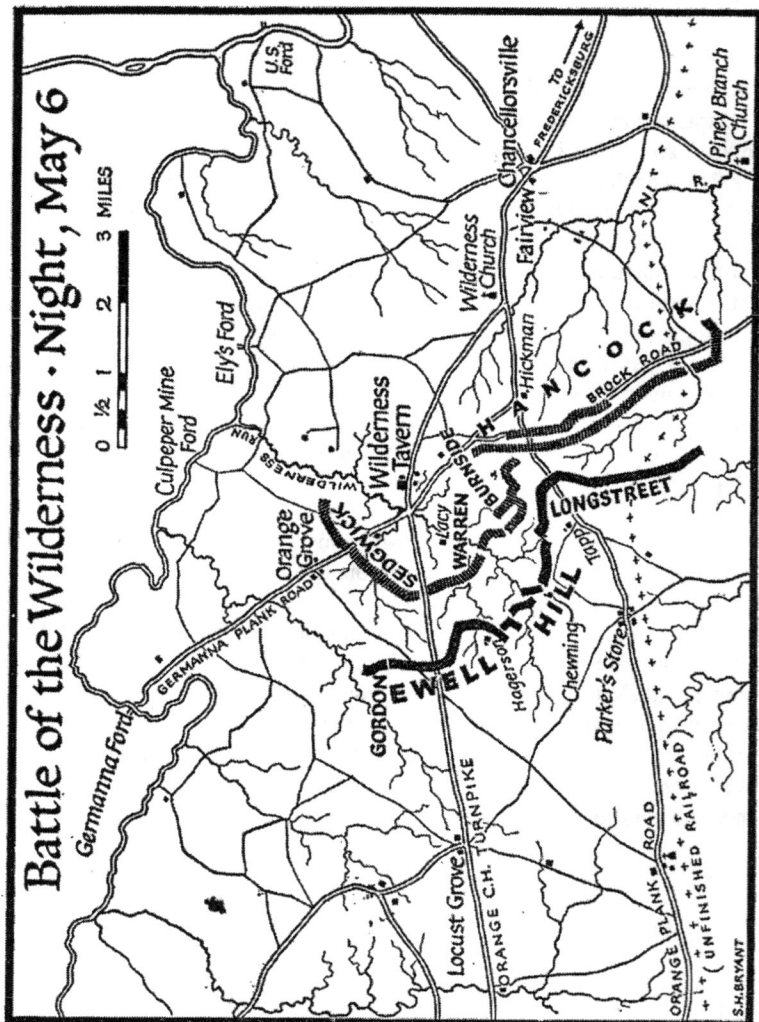

We continue with the Company A quotations.

"May 3, 1864, we are cooking rations, washing clothes and in general preparing to leave this area as the Yankees are coming and we are going to meet them this time and fight'em where we find'em or at least such is the talk of the camp. May 4th, 1864 with Heth's men finally gone, we fell in line of march behind them over familiar areas of march; that is, on

76

Orange Plank headed toward the tangled wooded forest of "the Wilderness". On May 5th, 1864 sporadic rifle fire and an occasional cannon shell was indication enough that the Yankee army was growing closer and closer. We left our heavier haversacks in wagons left behind at Parker's store and continued up the Orange Plank Road and into an area called "Widow Tapp Farms" and proceeded to the far left of our fast assembling army. Yankee rifle and shot was rapidly increasing although we could see them not but feeling their massive presence was a question settled by the old veterans who had the final word. That evening the Yankee army came on in mass attacking our main army located to our extreme right. Indeed Davis' Mississippi outfits were slowly falling back and one of General Hill's staff came on the run to direct us to their ranks to give aid and strength. We ran past the 13th and 14th South Carolina Regiments on their knees pleading for deliverance and speared deep into the Yankee held forest only to be recalled. Indeed, retreated back to our own lines crawling because rifle minnies were coming in every direction climbing limbs and rendering the pine trees bare of bark. We crawled toward southern voices in the dark and shot at northern sounding yells often only a few feet away. So thick and heavy were the forest entanglements in this area that no one could see far in any direction and didn't dare move throughout the night for fear of stumbling into the enemy. The slightest sneeze triggered hundreds of shots from every direction. About three in the morning of the 6th, a clear Yankee voice reasoned thus: I am Cake of the 96th Pennsylvania and our armies are mixed up. Come daylight, you and I know all hell will break loose and probably nobody in the sound of my voice will live to tell about it. You Rebs let us stand and move out and we will do likewise. Nobody answered but suddenly came alive with movement and men moving fast in whatever direction they felt best. And we moved back a hundred yards into the ranks of the 2nd Mississippi and survived to fight another day. Come daylight the Yankee army came on strong and hard which caused us to slowly retreat backward. The shot and shell would slowly eat up the woods in front of us causing our lines to seek the next batch to our rear to hide behind. Backwards we went and by half past six we had slowly retreated but nevertheless fighting up to a half mile from where we began this morning. We are losing the battle. Slowing Yankee movement was Bill Poague's artillery, Madison section commanded by a young hothead by name of Captain Richards (I think) who was double-shotting his cannon and firing over our retreating heads to the detriment of thousands of on rushing groups of enemy that were falling by the hundreds but still they came and if not for the arrival of Longstreet's men, we would have been taken by the enemy. But Longstreet's men filtered through our ranks at this early hour of seven and in this counter-attack sent the Yankees reeling and our command just sat down and rested from almost total exhaustion. But this rest was of one hour duration and we fell in column and ran ten minutes northward and into battle line and charged Yankee breastworks that were incomplete and overran the one assigned to us. But upon seeing hordes of enemy on rushers, we vacated this position and fell back onto a creek bed and here we fought off attack after attack until blessed nightfall descended and laid this nightmarish days work to an end. After dark we regrouped and up until midnight we dug trenches and built breastworks for the enemy attacks which would surely come in the morning. Enough moonlight displayed the horrors of hell as scary as any that could be imagined. Dead Yankees and our own were all over and every place to be seen. Hanging out of trees, half in and out of creeks - ruining the drinking water, even our own relatives had to be ignored in preparation for the coming morning battle. Never the less, come morning we would fight to the death and pull as many Yankees from among the land of the living as we possibly can. The butchers bill is high on this battle. Many have been captured including our own company Henry Jones and Alex Kelly who fell through the breastworks and were unable to run backwards to the creek bank. We watched helplessly at a distance as they were taken out and marched off the field. Captain John Mays, our company commander is badly wounded and helped from the field. Colonel Robert Folsom, shot in his side and chest removed by stretcher bearers to the ambulance wagon on Orange Plank Road. Richard P. Lester is now acting 14th commander and John Merrit is now acting company commander and we feel comfortable with both in these very trying moments. Joe Davis, Sam Ingrams, Andy Moran, Jim Riddle, and Bob Rogers are all wounded and gone with the ambulance wagon and not all will make it through the night. Saturday May 7th, we received little sleep due to the cannonading throughout the remaining night hours. It is drizzling rain. We waited for an attack which never came. At half past ten in the morning, General Hill came by looking very sickly himself as he was helped from his horse, and shook many hands and proceeded to do as much with the Mississippi regiment next to ours. We waited throughout the day with nothing happening outside of few shot and shell. Sunday, May 8th, 1864 remaining in position improving trenches and breastworks. Monday May 9th although the Yankee army seemed right in our front, much of our army began pulling out and heading south. No doubt the enemy is doing likewise as they lost heavily in the last three days."

Wilderness

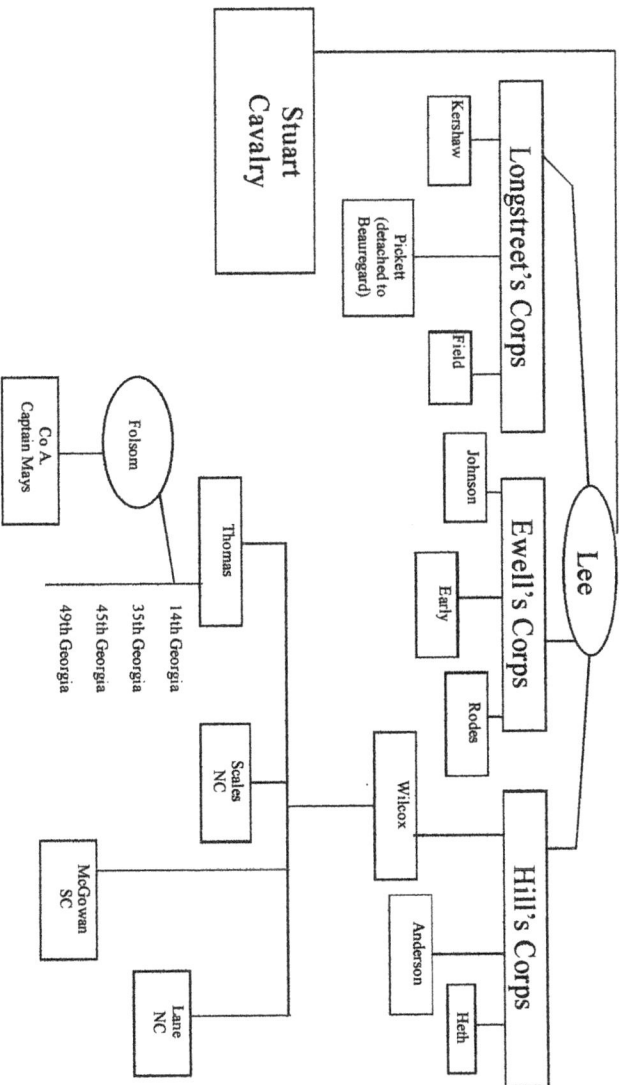

Lee

Longstreet's Corps
- Kershaw
- Pickett (detached to Beauregard)
- Field

Ewell's Corps
- Johnson
- Early
- Rodes

Hill's Corps
- Wilcox
  - Scales NC
  - McGowan SC
  - Thomas
    - Lane NC
    - Folsom
      - Co A Captain Mays
      - 14th Georgia
      - 35th Georgia
      - 45th Georgia
      - 49th Georgia
- Anderson
- Heth

Stuart Cavalry

The two-day battle of the Wilderness left Meade's Army in possession of Brock Road, but without the will to attack Lee's outnumbered army. With his usual superb reasoning Lee anticipated Grant's next move exactly, though this time perhaps the move was obvious. With possession of the Brock Road south to Spotsylvania and possession of the road southeast from Fredericksburg to Spotsylvania, Grant proposed to beat Lee to that crossroad town placing himself between Lee and Richmond, and thus to force Lee to attack him on Grant's selection of the battlefield. Lee could see that even without a good road south it was imperative to beat Grant to Spotsylvania as soon as Grant broke contact in the Wilderness.

Lee ordered his chief of artillery, General Pendleton, to cut a passage through the pine woods south to Spotsylvania. Leading Lee's engineers, Pendleton cut a four mile path going south from the Orange Plank Road to the Catharpin Road, which heads east into Spotsylvania. When Ewell's scouts reported the enemy's flank had broken contact with the Germana Ford crossing of the Rapidan late on 7 May, Lee knew for certain Grant was moving south. He directed Anderson to take command of Longstreet's I Corps and to lead the army south.

With Longstreet's serious wounds, Lee promoted R.H. Anderson from division command in Hill's Corps to command of I Corps. As it turned out, Hill reported sick during the night of 7-8 May. Lee hastily appointed Jubal Early, one of Ewell's division commanders, to temporary command of Hill's Corps. Gordon took Early's division command, with instant promotions on down the line in Ewell's Corps to fill subsequent brigade and regimental openings. Thus Lee entered the next phase of combat with two new corps commanders, two new division commanders, and several new leaders at brigade level.

In his first day at corps command, Anderson was about to make a lifetime of clutch decisions that would secure the important Spotsylvania crossroads for Lee. Lee's marching orders were for Anderson's Corps to move out at 3 AM on 8 May heading south via Pendleton's Trace, with Ewell's II Corps to follow by passing through III Corps, and finally with Early's (Hill's) III Corps to leave the Wilderness last to go south. When Anderson observed the primitive condition of Pendleton's "road" he disdained the six hours rest Lee's orders specified for his corps, and began moving his two divisions at 9 PM on 7 May. Those hours determined the course of the rest of the war in Virginia.

Marching in the dark over the crude trace, Anderson's Corps required eight hours to go eight miles to bring them east on the Catharpin Road just west of Spotsylvania at 5AM on 8 May. Observing no US forces in Spotsylvania, Anderson ordered a one hour break for rest and breakfast. At this hour, only Fitz Hugh Lee's division of Stuart's cavalry blocked the Brock Road just north of Spotsylvania. At 5 AM, they were engaged with Sheridan's cavalry coming south on the Brock Road followed closely by Warren's Corps of infantry. Without knowing it, Lee's cavalry provided Anderson's men the time for much needed rest and food by holding up Sheridan and Warren for one crucial hour. At the same time, Rosser's division of Stuart's cavalry battled Wilson's cavalry for possession of the road leading west from Fredericksburg into Spotsylvania.

Anderson became aware of the two separate cavalry engagements just as his men finished breakfast and just as Lee's outnumbered cavalry was being driven by Sheridan out of the woods and into clear fields of fire north of Spotsylvania. Anderson disregarded Rosser's action and threw Kershaw's two brigades in support of Lee. It was exactly the right decision. Kershaw moved up in support of Lee just as the four divisions of Warren's Corps arrived to assault what they thought was only cavalry. In the short fight that followed, Kershaw's division chewed up two of Warren's divisions and eliminated them from Meade's order of battle. Having saved the Brock Road approach to Spotsylvania, Anderson then moved in support of Rosser and secured Spotsylvania for Robert E. Lee's Army. By the margin of one hour and by perfect accidental timing, Anderson had beaten Meade to this important crossroads leading to Richmond. Dowdey's account in Lee's Last Campaign of the performance of Anderson and his corps that morning is about the best a military historian can hope to ever achieve.

Corps elements from both armies arrived at the battlefield site during 8 May. After his army had assembled, Lee's front stretched about four miles as depicted in the Spotsylvania map. For three days, Lee's Army prepared formidable earthwork defenses, which he became convinced Grant and Meade would not dare assault. By the night of 11 May Anderson's front faced north, Early's east, and Ewell's salient, known by the army as the Mule Shoe, projected northeast. Johnson's division of Ewell's Corps occupied the apex of the salient, with Wilcox' division of Early's Corps connecting on their immediate right.

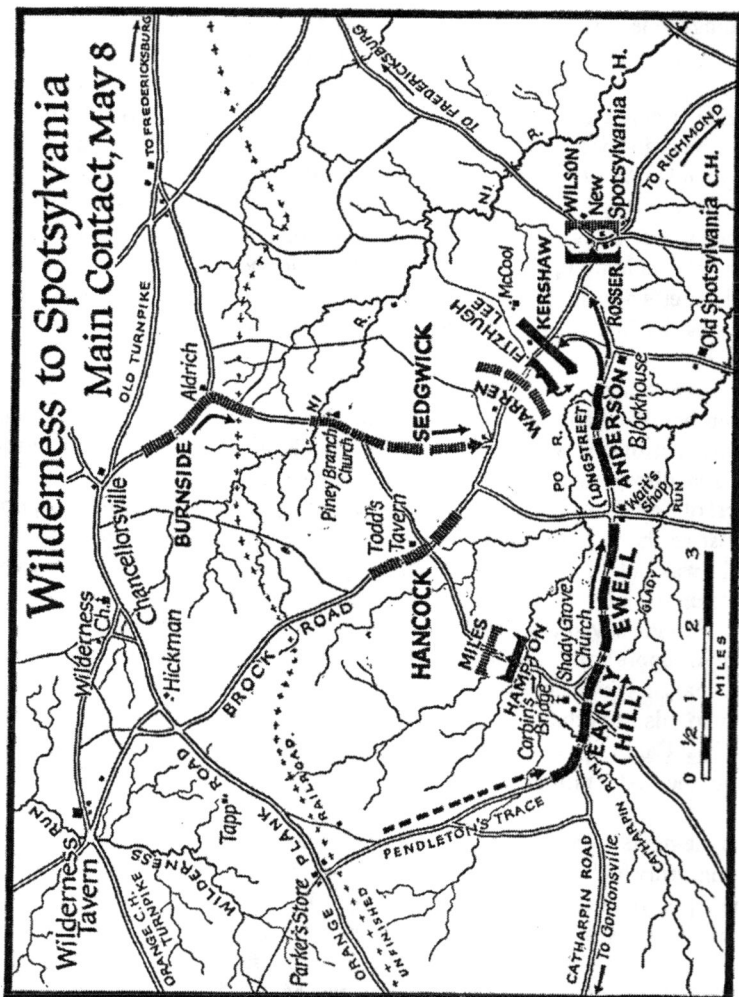

Looking at the detail of the Mule Shoe insert, we see Rode's and Johnson's divisions of Ewell's Corps occupied the front, with Gordon's division in support. Wilcox' division of Early's Corps connected on the immediate right placed in the order of brigade Lane, Thomas, Scales, and McGowan. Colonel Lester led the 14th GA regiment, and 1st Lt. John Merritt led A Company's 54 combatants. Heth's division extended the front southeast into Spotsylvania. Mahone's division of Early's Corps was on the complete opposite end of the line, across the Po River from Anderson.

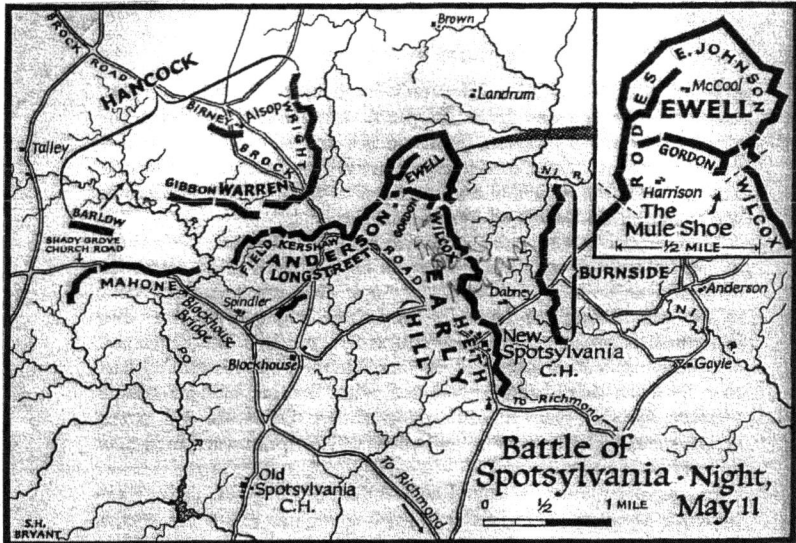

Battle of
Spotsylvania · Night,
May 11

Because of reports from his son's (Rooney Lee) cavalry division indicating Grant was pulling out again, Lee ordered the artillery moved from Johnson's Mule Shoe region of Ewell's Corps in preparation for a quick move south. Lee's deduction of Grant's decision to move was quite reasonable. Grant had not renewed his attacks in the Wilderness due to Lee's good field preparations. Now after three days of digging, the entrenchments at Spotsylvania were immeasurably better. Lee reasoned US forces would not attack him. Grant however was evolving a new determination - "We will fight it out on this line if it takes all summer."

In the foggy dawn of 12 May after an all-night rain, Hancock's four divisions hit Johnson's artillery-unsupported division at the apex of the salient. Johnson's two Virginia brigades were over run in minutes. Lee's Army was cut in two, with Rodes' right flank exposed and Wilcox' left flank exposed. In this early morning emergency, there was absolutely no time for Lee, Ewell, and Early to coordinate action to save the army. Several of Lee's junior generals took the initiative and independently produced immediate action to close the gap.

83

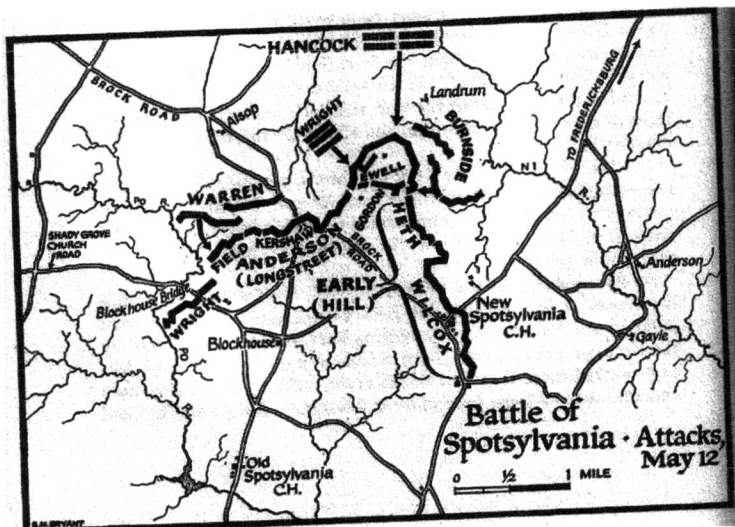

Battle of
Spotsylvania · Attacks,
May 12

On the left Ramseur wheeled about his North Carolina brigade of Rodes' division and charged. From the secondary line Gordon charged his two-brigade division of Virginians and Georgians. On the right, Lane bent his North Carolina brigade at right angles to face the sudden appearance of the new enemy on his left flank. Wilcox pulled Thomas and Scales out of line to support Lane and to provide enfilade fire into the four US divisions that now occupied Ewell's center. Together, these six brigades from three separate divisions and two separate corps drove four US divisions out of the salient to reestablish the original dawn line.

The two armies fought in the salient for all of the rest of that rainy day. Ewell has been severely criticized as a corps commander during the 1864 campaign, but his corps fought this day with fierce determination. Somehow the soldiers on both sides seemed to take individual and personal responsibility to destroy the enemy. Bruce Catton gives the US perspective of the 12 May fighting in A Stillness at Appomattox, and Clifford Dowdey gives the Confederate perspective in Lee's Last Campaign. The soldiers fought with complete disregard for personal safety, as the intense desire to kill the enemy appears to have exceeded the level attained at any other time in the war. "Nothing in the war equaled the ferocity at the Bloody Angle (Mule Shoe) of Spotsylvania, not even the peak of Pickett's charge at Gettysburg"- Hansen, The Civil War.

Ewell's and Early's men fought all day and night to gain time while Lee's engineers fortified the secondary line that Gordon's men had occupied that morning. Quoting from Dowdey:

"Lee held his somnambulistic men at the grisly parapet (apex of the salient) until a new line was completed along the base of the salient. During that endless day of the 12th, men were put to work as long as they could stand. For the rush job on the new line across the base of the salient, connecting with Early's Corps on the right and the southwest segment of Rodes' line on the left, Lee collected during the afternoon all detached units and all the men from engaged units who were out of the lines for one reason or another and they completed the straight line by mid-night. Then the shattered, half-conscience men lurched their way back to the new works, where they fell out on the muddy ground, nearer dead than alive. Grant's men also withdrew, and the unmanned fortifications of the old Mule Shoe embraced only a triangular section of the ghostly woods."

As the 12 May map shows, all four of Warren's, Wright's, Burnside's, and Hancock's Corps of Meade's Army assaulted Lee's lines. After Wilcox wheeled to fire into the salient, Early moved Heth's division in to close the hole left by Wilcox. By the end of the day Wilcox had moved his exhausted division out to Heth's former position – only to be assaulted then by Burnside's Corps. Mahone moved his division across the Po in support of Ewell. The day ended with Lee's Army secure along a continuous front in which Ewell's Corps finally gave up the salient and fell back to the secondary line that the Confederate engineers, and anyone else Lee could grab, had finished.

Fighting would continue for the next seven days until Grant gave up and ordered Meade on yet another flank movement south. AJ's Company A of the 14th suffered comparatively light casualties in the eight days of Spotsylvania. Pvt. William Reuben suffered an amputated leg, Sgt. Hiram Jones was wounded, and Pvt. William Banks was wounded in his shoulder but would return for battle at Petersburg. Overall the 14th sustained a heavier toll, exceeding 10% casualties. Twenty-two were killed, 23 wounded, and 28 were captured. Lee's total casualties ran near 10,000 - largely from Johnson's shattered division. Meade's Army was jolted by a casualty figure of 17,000. In two prolonged engagements with Lee, Grant had lost one-third of Meade's infantry.

Spotsylvania

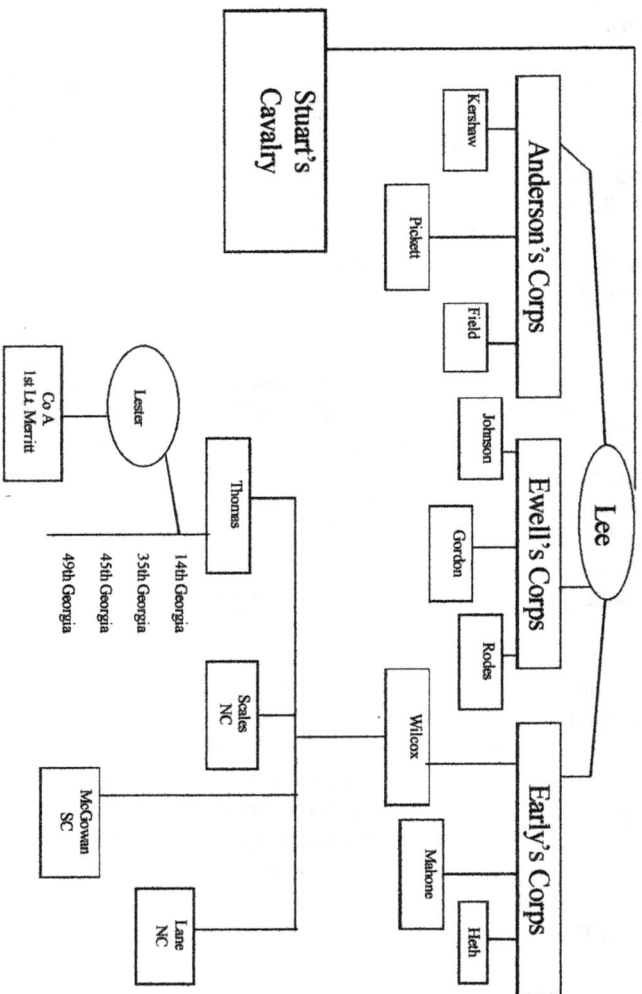

Stuart's Cavalry

Lee

Anderson's Corps
- Kershaw
- Pickett
- Field

Ewell's Corps
- Johnson
- Gordon
- Rodes

Early's Corps
- Mahone
- Heth

Wilcox
- Scales NC
- McGowan SC
- Lane NC

Thomas
- Lester
  - Co A 1st Lt. Merritt
- 14th Georgia
- 35th Georgia
- 45th Georgia
- 49th Georgia

The 14th GA eyewitness to the Spotsylvania fighting was limited and to the point.

"About three o'clock in the evening we began arriving at the Spotsylvania Courthouse area. Crossing Brock Road, we headed into the field east of that city. The town's people were furious that we were seeking confrontation with yankees here instead of elsewhere. But it mattered not as shells were beginning to fall and refugees were leaving southward thus jamming roads with wagons and cattle tied to one another. May 11th, 1864 - with our trenches and other fortified positions completed, we wait in the drizzling rain for the enemy. The rain increased to torrents at nightfall. The enemy became aware of our presence and gathered also, which included the 4th Corps under Burnside. Thursday, May 12th, 1864- the enemy went on the attack against Lane's men stationed next to us (14th GA) and was pushing the 28th North Carolina back on top of us and we merged into their ranks and together drove the enemy from the field taking several hundred prisoners. For the remainder of the day and night was constant onslaught by them, then counter-attacks by us. Tooth and nail and hand to hand combat ensued as thousands on both sides would head into each other with bayonets and attempts to stick each other through the log spaces. Cannon from both sides was rushed to within fifty yards of this mass assembly and fired point blank into the opposing ranks opening wide gaps, only to observe them filling in again. Friday, May 13th evolved into slow but constant skirmishing between the armies but a respectful distance in-between. Saturday, May 14th, 1864- provided a great lull and rains continued. The ditch of running water from the direction northward was literally running red with what appeared to be pure blood from the wounded tending themselves."

RETREAT TO PETERSBURG

On 19 May 1864 Grant directed Meade to begin breaking contact with Lee's Army. Both armies moved out a corps at a time. Hill's Corps moved out last at 9 PM on 21 May. From 4 May until 19 May, there had not been one hour where some portion of the front between the two armies was not engaged. For 15 days, both sides had been alert for instantaneous action. Grant's maneuver south must have been welcome to both sides. In the last hours of skirmishing on the 21st, the 14th suffered one death, one wounding, and one captured - none from Company A.

On the 21st, Lee guessed correctly that Grant would attempt to cross the North Anna River near Hanover Junction, just 22 miles north of Richmond. Marching on interior lines, Lee's Army beat Meade across the river at Jericho and Ox Fords. Lee established lines on the 22nd running west to east – in sequence by corps Hill, Anderson, and Ewell - along the south bank of the North Anna. Wilcox' division occupied the extreme left of the line. Lt. Colonel Lester now commanded the 14th GA, and First Lieutenant Merritt commanded Company A, now depleted to a strength of 59. From this date on, Lee's lack of faith in his corps commanders would greatly influence the battlefield. With Longstreet wounded, Lee had no corps commander whom he felt he could trust to manage a field, and Lee himself was about to come down ill.

On the afternoon of 23 May, Warren's Corps of Meade's Army was the first to cross the North Anna River at Jericho Ford facing Hill's front. Hill's Corps, having no rest from marching or fighting since 4 May, attacked Warren at 1800 on 23 May. Lee had intended that Hill hit Warren as he crossed the river – his most vulnerable time. Instead Hill was slow to act, and his corps attacked after Warren had completed his crossing. Wilcox' division alone attacked four US divisions. Thomas' brigade led the assault, hitting Cutler's division. Thomas had initial success, pushing Cutler's division back toward the river. But against greatly superior numbers, the attack failed. The 14th Georgia suffered one death, two wounded, and five captured. Company A suffered no casualties. Hill's Corps fell back a couple miles, allowing Wright to join Warren south of the river on Meade's right.

The next day Lee was publicly enraged with Hill for attacking with only Wilcox' division, asking "Why did you not do as Jackson would have done - thrown your whole force upon those people and driven them back?" But even with Hill's failure to destroy Warren, Lee's front was still in excellent condition to strike a great blow on Meade's Army.

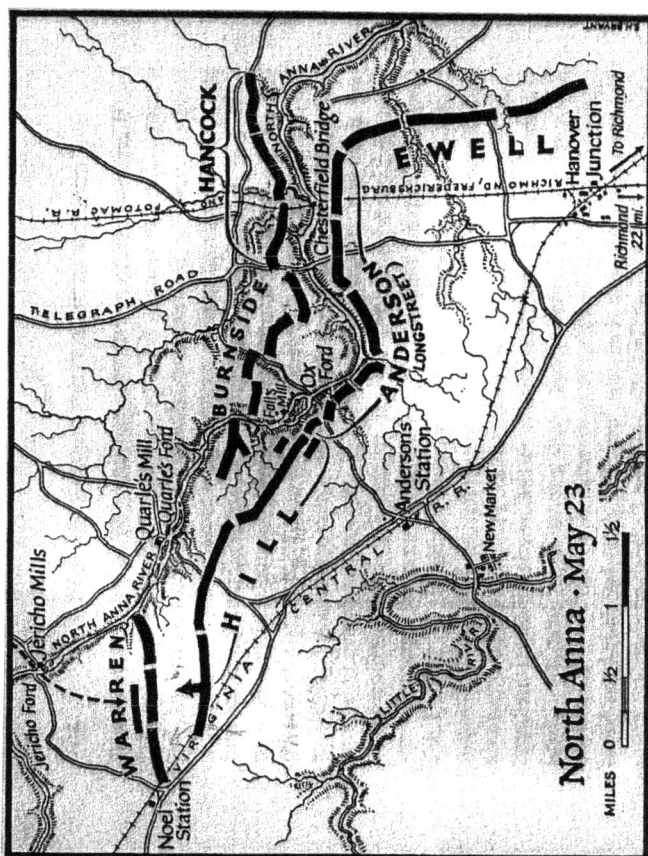

With Hill and Anderson well dug in, Lee laid plans for Ewell's Corps to spring
the trap in one of his best opportunities of the war. On the 24th, he pulled Ewell
back from the North Anna to the Richmond and Fredericksburg railroad track,
allowing Hancock to cross the river at the Chesterfield Bridge. Lee planned to
hit Hancock south of the river in completely unprepared positions. To save
Hancock; Wright, Warren, and Burnside would have had to fight through Hill's
and Anderson's dug-in corps or to cross the river twice. Both armies agreed
later this was one of the war's historic opportunities. Lee unfortunately fell
extremely ill on the 24th and would not trust any of his three corps commanders
to manage the complex troop movements of his plan. Had Longstreet or
Jackson been present, Lee would undoubtedly have yielded the field.

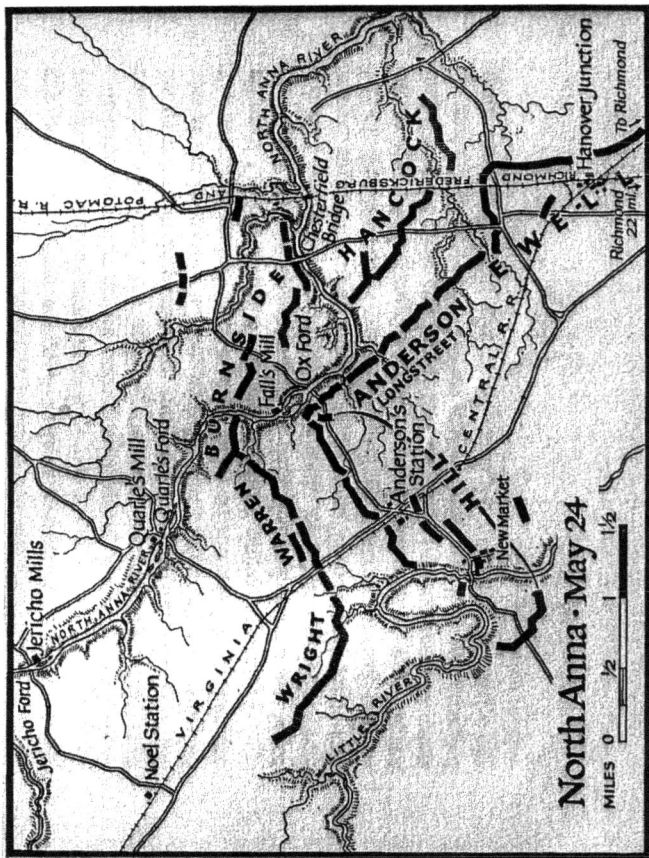

Lee remained sick for three days, and on the 27th Hancock finally withdrew. Grant moved Meade's Army east and south across the Pamunkey River. Lee could only counter by moving to Cold Harbor to stay between Meade and Richmond. On this day Ewell reported sick. Early took command of Ewell's Corps and ultimately relieved Ewell permanently. Quotations from the 14th GA writer continue.

North Anna River

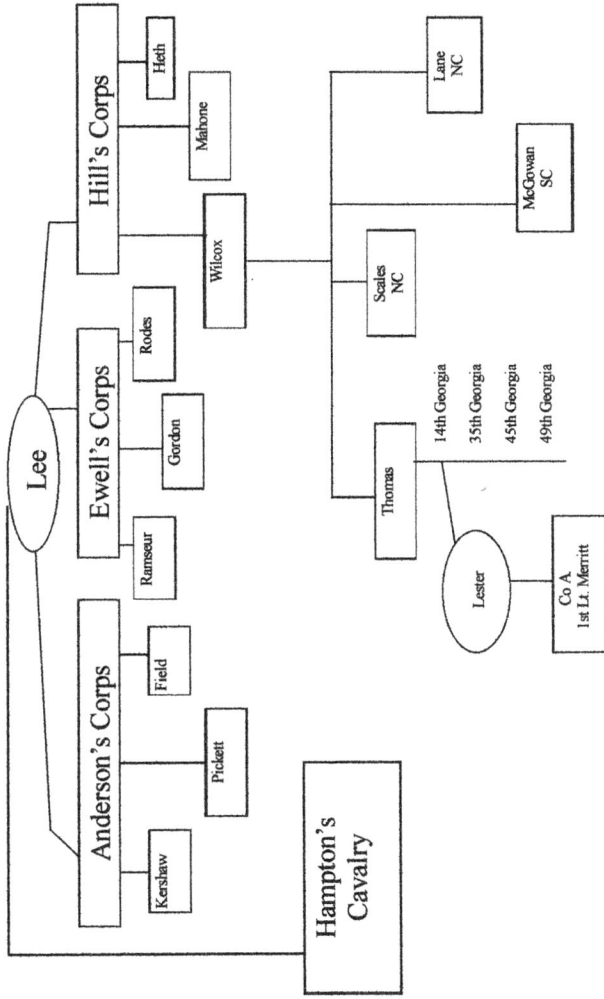

Lee

Anderson's Corps
- Kershaw
- Pickett
- Field

Ewell's Corps
- Ramseur
- Gordon
- Rodes

Hill's Corps
- Mahone
- Heth
- Wilcox
  - Scales NC
    - Thomas
      - 14th Georgia
      - 35th Georgia
      - 45th Georgia
      - 49th Georgia
      - Lester
        - Co A 1st Lt. Merritt
  - McGowan SC
  - Lane NC

Hampton's Cavalry

"Sunday, May 15th. Weather became clear and pleasant and our dead were being placed in mass graves which at times was to risk injury from the enemy's distant sharpshooters. The lull and burials continued day after day until the 21st at which time we gathered and marched away leaving many of the dead unburied; indeed the rotting flesh around the Courthouse area was unbearable. Nevertheless, Grant was pulling out on his side and we suppose Bobby Lee means to keep our army between the yankees and Richmond. On the late evening we start our march southward and did so throughout the night arriving on the North Anna River at mid-day on the 22nd of May, 1864. Begin deploying to form battle lines near Jericho Mills. Thus arranged, we charge northward driving the Yankee's Bucktail Brigade and their famed Iron Brigade before us into very disorderly retreat. But suddenly cannon and shot from high ground sent the Thomas Brigade into full retreat backward. May 27th, Friday we again pull out marching southward and finally into the Totopotomi Creek area near Shady Grove Church Road and built elaborate ditches to receive Mr. Grant but upon viewing these fortifications, General Grant continued his line of march around our army and continued southward. So did our army."

Meade beat Lee south of the Pamunkey and then blew the initiative himself by entrenching instead of driving on to Richmond. The delay resulted in the two armies squaring off and digging in. Lee attacked with Anderson's Corps on the 31st. Lee was disappointed with Anderson's performance, and the attack failed. Meade then extended his lines further south to the Chickahominy to stretch Lee as thin as possible.

By the night of 2 June, Lee's lines stretched six miles from the Totopotomi Creek to the Chickahominy River. Hill's divisions occupied opposite ends. From north to south the units ran Heth's division, Early's three divisions, Anderson's three divisions, Hoke's division that had been detached from Beauregard, Breckenridges two independent brigades (that had joined Lee on the 31st), and Wilcox' division. Wilcox occupied the extreme right, anchoring Lee's line at the Grapevine Bridge, which recall Porter had used to escape A. P. Hill's, D. H. Hill's and Longstreet's attacks at Gaines Mill on 27 June 1862.

Cold Harbor

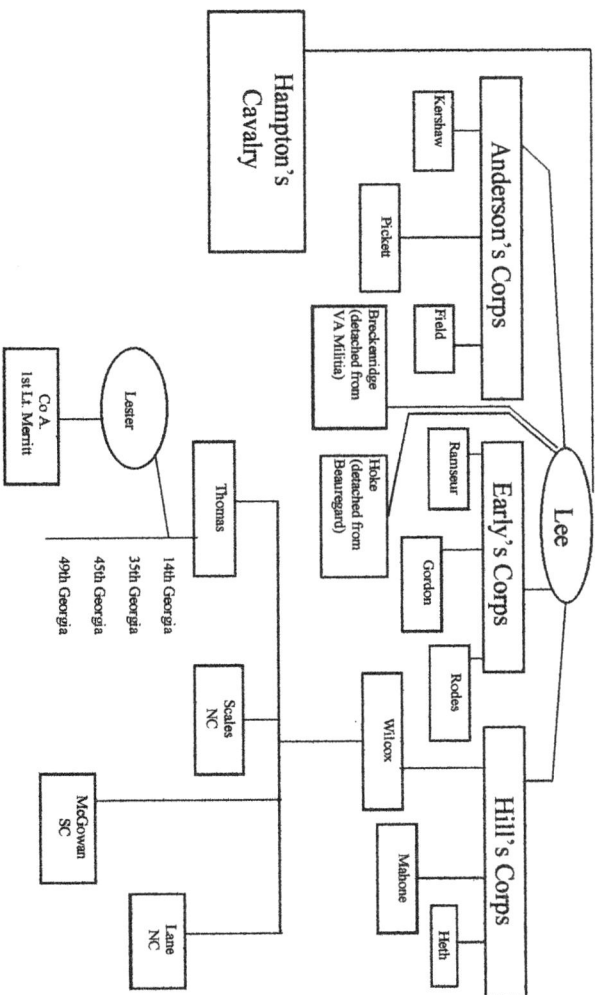

Lee

- Hampton's Cavalry
- Anderson's Corps
  - Kershaw
  - Pickett
  - Field
  - Breckenridge (detached from VA Militia)
- Early's Corps
  - Hoke (detached from Beauregard)
  - Ramseur
  - Gordon
  - Rodes
- Hill's Corps
  - Wilcox
    - Thomas
      - 14th Georgia
      - 35th Georgia
      - 45th Georgia
      - 49th Georgia
    - Scales NC
    - McGowan SC
    - Lane NC
  - Mahone
  - Heth

Lester
Co A. 1st Lt. Merritt

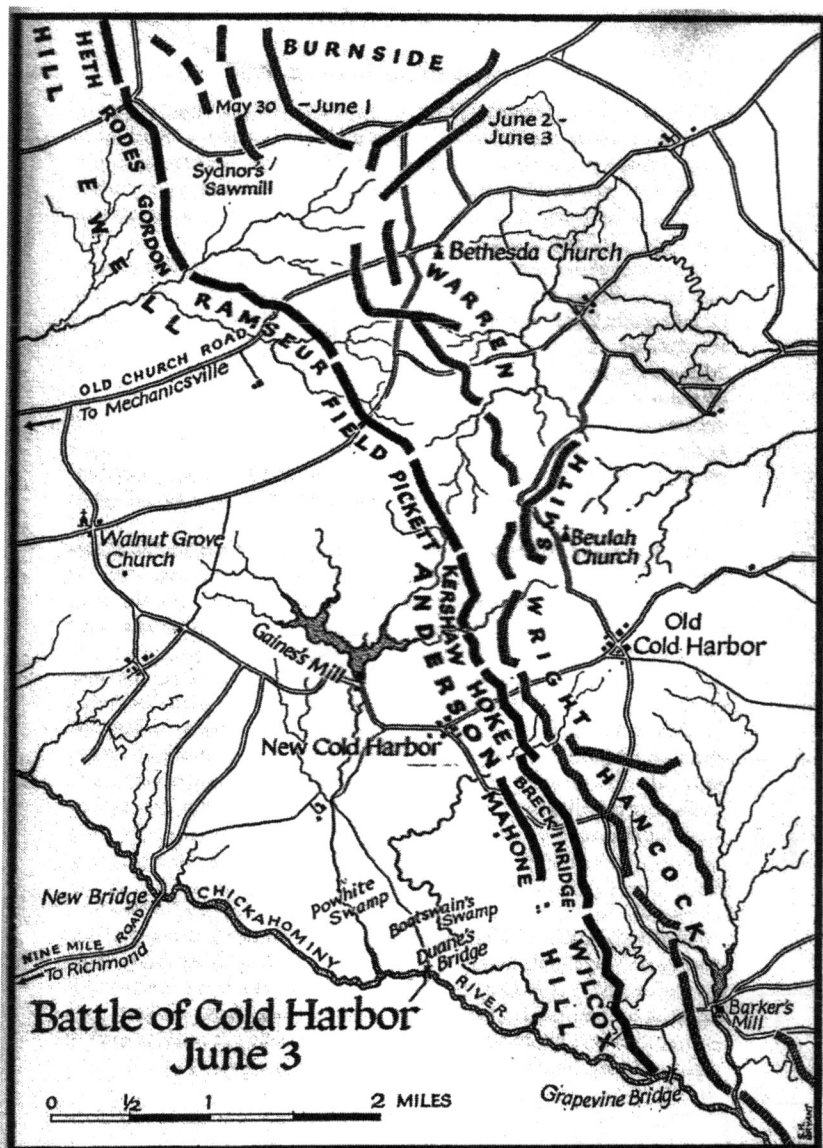

Battle of Cold Harbor
June 3

0   ½   1   2 MILES

94

On the night of 2 June, Lee's troops were well prepared but very thin. Mahone was placed in support of Breckenridge, but otherwise over the whole six miles not one regiment was held in reserve. The line waited confidently in a driving rainstorm for an attack expected in the early morning.

Instead of concentrating its forces for attack at a single point, the US line advanced along almost the entire front at Cold Harbor in an attack that began about 0430 on 3 June. The battle was over in less than one half hour. In the first eight minutes over 7,000 US casualties fell in killed and wounded. Thousands were pinned down within a couple hundred yards of the Confederate line. Wounded and unwounded lay all day in the blazing heat. To move from cover or concealment invited death. US officers could not induce additional attack waves to assault Lee's line. The front lay stalemated all day on the 3rd. At nightfall those who could, retreated to safety.

Company A suffered no casualties in this destruction of the US assault at Cold Harbor. The regiment lost five captured, four wounded, and no deaths. The writer below describes the pounding they gave the US forces.

"On June 1st, we beat off minor attacks with the aid of well placed artillery. June 2nd, 1864 Wednesday we entrenched with some unusual zigzag type fortifications laid out by our engineers to receive a superior force. Cold Harbor crossroads was nearby. Hard downpours of rain continued that evening and throughout the night rendering it difficult to walk up and down our mud filled ditches. Friday, June 3rd, 1864- at 4:30 AM, Grant's army attacked head-on. It was an all-out attempt to overrun and secure us for his own. But it worked not. Instead our artillery and flanking movements worked in beautiful coordination and before our lines fell a massive number. Slaughter of enemy onrushes became an act of pitiful futility on their part. Our lines, as far as the eye could see, were having similar successes and the Yankee lines ever came forward in a seeming trance-like death wish, which they received in great abundance. This continued until half past noon, then slacked off to a lull. The countryside in our front was so thickly strewn with blue uniforms as to constitute a continuous connected carpet across the landscape. After that, we settled into our trenches for endless cannonading from the enemy with light skirmishing which continued until June 12th."

At the beginning of the war, both armies used frontal assault with limited success. By 1864 defenders had learned to entrench well, and from Cold Harbor on, assaulting fortified lines was considered mostly hopeless. Thus after 3 June at Cold Harbor, neither Lee nor Grant dared attack. The lines remained stalemated for ten days.

Greatly outnumbered and with his back to Richmond, Lee could not risk maneuver, and was constrained to yield the initiative to Grant and Meade. On the 14th Grant moved Warren's Corps south to Riddle's Shop, southeast of Richmond. Hill and Anderson's Corps marched to confront him at Malvern Hill and for two days prepared for an attack that never came. Early, with Ewell's Corps, was sent north to the Shenandoah Valley to threaten Washington as Jackson had done in 1862.

Screened by Warren at Riddle's Shop, Hancock, Wright, Smith, and Burnside marched to the James and crossed to attack Petersburg. For two days Lee did not know where the bulk of Meade's Army was. He and Beauregard (with little cooperation) tried to figure Meade's next move. Suddenly on the 16th 80,000 of Meade's Army appeared east of Petersburg, with only Beauregard's Army of 10,000 to defend this important railroad junction. On the 17th Lee raced A. P. Hill's Corps to Beauregard's rescue. Hill's Corps supported Beauregard by crossing the James at Chaffin's Bluff and rushing south to Beauregard's rear. But Beauregard fought the crucial battle of Petersburg on June 17th outnumbered eight to one.

Beauregard's Army was a composite of Virginia militia, inexperienced North Carolina troops, and a sprinkling of veterans from Lee and the West. For the entire day of the 17th they fought four of Meade's veteran corps to a standstill. Probably no group of Confederate defenders can claim a more shining performance against such forces. The US forces were able to gain the outer eastern trenches, but could not obtain possession of the city or of the railroad yards.

The march of A. P. Hill's Corps to the rescue at Petersburg has been likened to a death march. Unit integrity was not deemed important in comparison with the mission to get there. Stragglers were simply left behind. Without doubt, the training received as Jackson's "foot cavalry" paid big dividends this day as the weary troops pushed themselves in the dusty June heat. Wilcox' division reached the Petersburg battlefield in the late afternoon. Meade had shortly before ordered a general assault against Petersburg with each of his corps commanders counseled to act independently. With the arrival of the totally exhausted Confederate troops, US veteran troops realized the golden opportunity to capture Petersburg was now lost. One US corps attempting to flank Beauregard to the west was cut off by Heth's division. Another US unit set to assault Wilcox late in the day bogged down. A green regiment rose to renew the charge and was shouted down by a more experienced group.

After a few days of rest in the trenches, U.S. Major General Warren's V Corps attempted to extend the front west of Jerusalem Plank Road. Beauregard later admitted such a move on the 17th would have defeated him. On the 21st Wilcox' division came out of their lines and attacked Birney's division of Warren's Corps. The demoralized enemy was easily defeated, netting over a whole brigade of prisoners. This one sided victory cost the 14th no casualties, though they inflicted many. Such was a measure of the relative fighting capabilities of the two armies at this point.

Despite their confidence in Robert E. Lee, many of Thomas's Georgians worried about the situation in their home state. In early May 1864, a US Army under William T. Sherman had advanced deep into northwest Georgia, forcing the Confederate Army there under Joseph E. Johnston southward toward Atlanta. Private Chancely undoubtedly spoke for Jack Dewberry when he wrote home that "you may be assured that most of the Georgians are wanting to come and protect their own state," but Chancely explained that "a soldier don't get what he wants by a great deal."

Several weeks later, Chancely again expressed his concern about Joseph E. Johnston's strategy of retreating, telling his cousin that "I think old Johnson will [retreat] down to Monroe [County] before he stop . . . I don't like this . . . fighting in Virginia and letting the yankees run all over Georgia." Many other men in the 14th Georgia, including Jack Dewberry, probably agreed with Chancely when he claimed that he would "rather fight for those that I love."

William F. Chancely wrote home on June 19 from the position Thomas's Brigade had taken south of Petersburg. "They made an attack on our lines just as we got here yesterday but did not succeed in doing any harm," he explained, "we whipped them and sent them back in confusion." Chancely also testified that he "never saw the men in better spirits in my life considering the hard marches that we have to endure."

On the 28th of June, the 14th was released from the Petersburg, Virginia, lines and transferred to picket duty on the Rapidan. No doubt this was a welcome change. After ten days, they returned to the Petersburg lines. On 30 July, the 14th Georgia occupied the eastern most trenches, adjacent to the Appomattox River. Thus they missed the Battle of the Crater, in which Burnside's Corps attempted to breach Lee's fortified lines by allowing former Pennsylvania miners to excavate a tunnel under them. The plan was to load this tunnel with tons of high explosives and blow a sufficiently wide gap to allow an unstoppable invasion through the breach. This resulted in yet another defeat for Meade's Army and in the permanent retirement of Burnside from the army.

Since the bloody days at Spotsvlvania, the 14th GA had marched nearly 100 miles and fought two major engagements and two lesser ones. It had assisted Lee to deflect Grant at the North Anna River and to repulse Grant at Cold Harbor, had dug in against Grant's deception at Riddle's Shop, had raced in exhaustion to help Beauregard save Petersburg, and had inflicted huge losses on Warren's Corps at Petersburg. All of these were accomplished with but 17 total casualties (about 3%). We pick up on the 14th GA narrative at June 15th.

"On June 15th, we went in search of the enemy and marched into the White Oak area and encountered yankee cavalry, many of whom were captured. June 18th, 1864 the enemy had melted out of existence and reports indicated Petersburg, Virginia is under attack. Throughout the day we crossed over the river at Chaffin' Bluff and later continued on an extremely hard march down the Petersburg turnpike. There were many sick among us for lack of food and rest which severely weakened us this past month and a half, and this forty mile march to save the city of Petersburg in the extreme heat, may be likened to a death march which many were unable to accomplish and simply straggled in days later. Nevertheless, the main body continued on arriving late in the evening. June 19th, 1864 rested somewhat but nevertheless improved entrenchments southeast of Petersburg. General Beauregard is being heralded as today's hero for holding the lines until reinforcements arrived. June 21st, 1864. It being rumored the yankee General Birney was building a fort a few miles south of the city, we headed in the evening in that direction west of Jerusalem Plank Road and attacked. The enemy was already disorganized and unprepared but our good fortunes netted four good artillery pieces and perhaps two thousand prisoners. June 28th, 1864. Some Mississippi outfits relieved us in the trenches and we went by rail to Richmond, and then beyond to the Rapidan for picket duty. July 8th, 1864 we returned to Petersburg to the same area. July 13th, 1864. Marched up to the northeast side of Petersburg on the Appomattox River. July 30th, 1864 a terrific explosion to the south of us with massive amounts of black smoke boiling upward high into the morning sky of a quarter before five o'clock. The nearby cavalry mounted to run in that direction. Our curiosity at a peak, it was a heavy conversation piece for days. Although neither our brigade or regiments was near the area, still the rumors were wild with multiple fantacies. That afternoon the Virginia cavalry unit returned explaining the yankees had blown up a portion of our line by tunneling under but had been repulsed with heavy losses. Some of our men braved shell and rifle fire just to go down and look at this amazing thing and while there aided the wounded and buried dead in the hundreds."

Somehow the eight-month siege of Petersburg worked wonderfully for Grant's and Lincoln's cause. Whether by design or accident is not clear, but morale in the two armies completely reversed over this time period. At the end of August 1864, Lee's Army was flush with pride of tactical success. From the Wilderness to Petersburg, they had not been defeated on any battlefield. They had inflicted enormous casualties on Meade's Army, and had recent victories at Cold Harbor, Petersburg, and the Crater. Meade's Army conversely was becoming demoralized. Since May it had suffered 80,000 casualties. True it was still at full strength from new recruiting and conscription, but many of the new men were low-lifes that would not have been tolerated in a peacetime army. Meades' veterans believed they were better off without them. Johnston's Army still held Atlanta, and Jubal Early actually threatened Washington. In late summer, Lincoln expected defeat in the fall elections, probably accompanied by a negotiated peace with a recognized Confederacy.

Despair set in that winter, and the feelings of the Dewberrys were probably similar to those of Lieutenant Wiley J. Smith of the 14th Georgia. On January 23, 1865, Smith wrote home that "I think if there is not something done some where else that next summer will finish what few of us . . . is left in this army." "We have got the whole Yankee army yes the whole Yankee nation to fight," exclaimed Smith, "but I am going to stay and fight them as long as there is any Southern soldiers in the field." Lieutenant Smith had never seen the men as "low spirited in my life" and it had been six months since either the officers or men had received pay. The men got short rations, Smith told his wife, "but make out better I am afraid than you . . . at home."

By March 1865 Lee's Army was reduced by one-third with desertions and furloughs of indulgence. Sherman had captured Atlanta and devastated a good portion of Georgia. Sheridan had torched the Shenandoah Valley of Virginia. Food was short for much of the Confederacy and for both of its main armies. The temptations to desert must have been great for the Georgia regiments with the uncertainties at home, and for the Virginia regiments, where home was frequently so close. By March, Meade's Army sensed an opportunity to wrap things up and win the war. Many were anxious to fight.

For the eight months of the Petersburg siege, the lengths of the two lines presented an interesting contrast. On the eastern end, lines ran south from the Appomattox River and were only about 200 yards apart. Quoting Bruce Catton in A Stillness At Appomattox, "here the two armies played for keeps. Sharpshooters and artillery gunners kept a constant vigil on both sides, and it was generally considered certain death to expose oneself for more than a moment." About two miles from the river the lines turned west and ran several miles, diverging as much as two miles apart.

From here west the men of both armies observed an informal truce and fraternized often when general officers were not present. When officers approached, the enemies would actually warn each other. One day when US General Crawford stood on a parapet to observe the Confederate lines, some US pickets received a hand written note from the Confederate pickets stating "tell the fellow with the spy glass to clear out or we shall have to shoot him."

That was the front. It was so well entrenched and enfiladed that there was not the least chance that either side could storm the other. Therefore the standoff continued for many long months, while Confederate fortunes degraded in the West, and food shortages heightened East and West. Demoralization was unavoidable in Lee's Army. Desertions could not be stopped, but perhaps were reduced by extended leaves of indulgence granted liberally.

The 14th Georgia was no exception with regard to desertions, leaves, and unauthorized absences. The 14th conducted its last regimental roll call on 28 February 1865. Company A has none listed as deserted, but five soldiers are listed as absent without leave on this roster. Two soldiers are listed as on furloughs of indulgence - no later record, and two are listed as sick in hospital - no later record. Captain John Merritt and Pvt. Berry W. Dewberry are listed as on furlough of indulgence, both listed as having reached Danville, Virginia on returning from furlough when the war ended. Pvt's D. M. Sanford and R. W. Riddle were discharged due to disability in August and September 1864. Pvt. Dorsey died in the Richmond Hospital in spring 1865. These losses left Company A at a strength of 44. Captain Merritt had command of the company (though he was not present when the March fighting started), and Colonel Lester commanded the regiment. The brigade was so depleted it appeared more like a regiment.

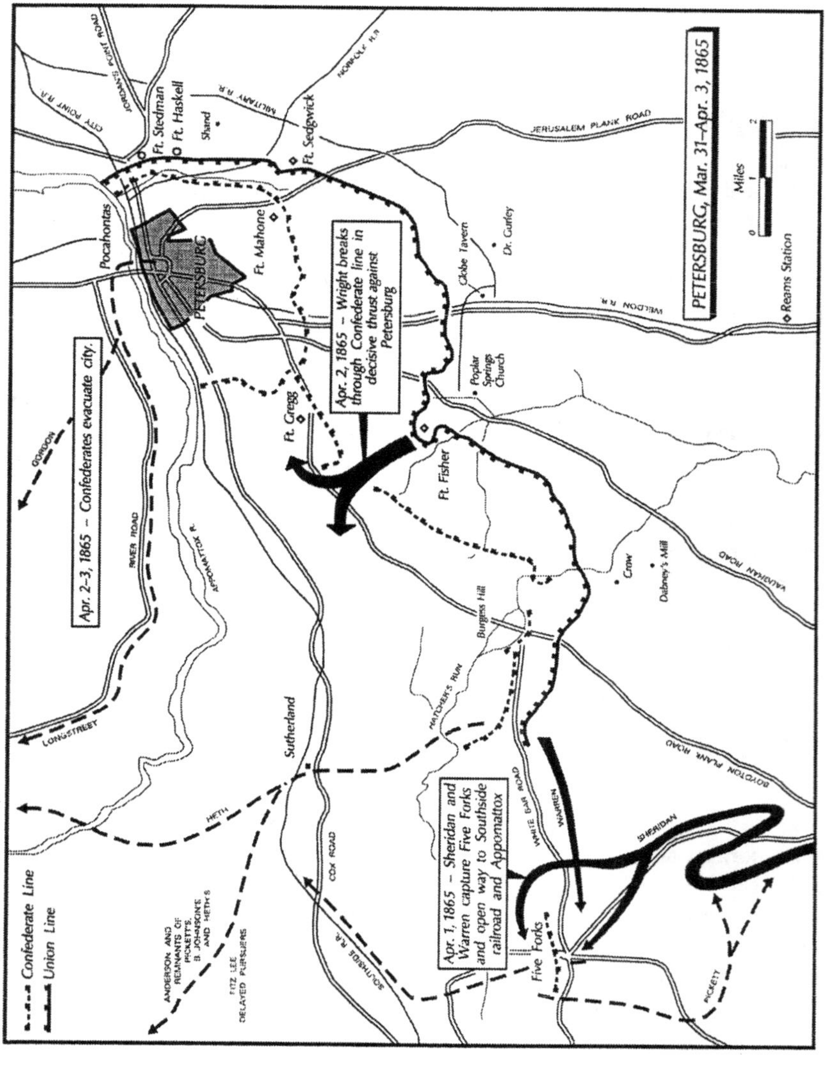

PETERSBURG, Mar. 31–Apr. 3, 1865

Miles

◆ Reams Station

Apr. 2, 1865 – Wright breaks through Confederate line in decisive thrust against Petersburg

Apr. 2–3, 1865 – Confederates evacuate city.

Apr. 1, 1865 – Sheridan and Warren capture Five Forks and open way to Southside railroad and Appomattox

∎▪▪▪ Confederate Line
▬▬▬ Union Line

CITY POINT R.R.
APPOMATTOX POINT ROAD
Ft. Stedman
Ft. Haskell
Stand
MILITARY R.R.
NORFOLK R.R.
Ft. Sedgwick
JERUSALEM PLANK ROAD
Globe Tavern
Dr. Gurley
WELDON R.R.
Pocahontas
PETERSBURG
Ft. Mahone
Ft. Gregg
Poplar Springs Church
GORDON
RIVER ROAD
APPOMATTOX R.
Ft. Fisher
Crow
Dabney's Mill
VAUGHAN ROAD
LONGSTREET
Sutherland
HETH
COX ROAD
Burgess Hill
HATCHER'S RUN
BOYDTON PLANK ROAD
TO SHERIDAN
ANDERSON AND REMNANTS OF PICKETT'S B. JOHNSON'S AND HETH'S
FITZ LEE DELAYED PURSUERS
SOUTHSIDE R.R.
WHITE OAK ROAD
WARREN
Five Forks
PICKETT

102

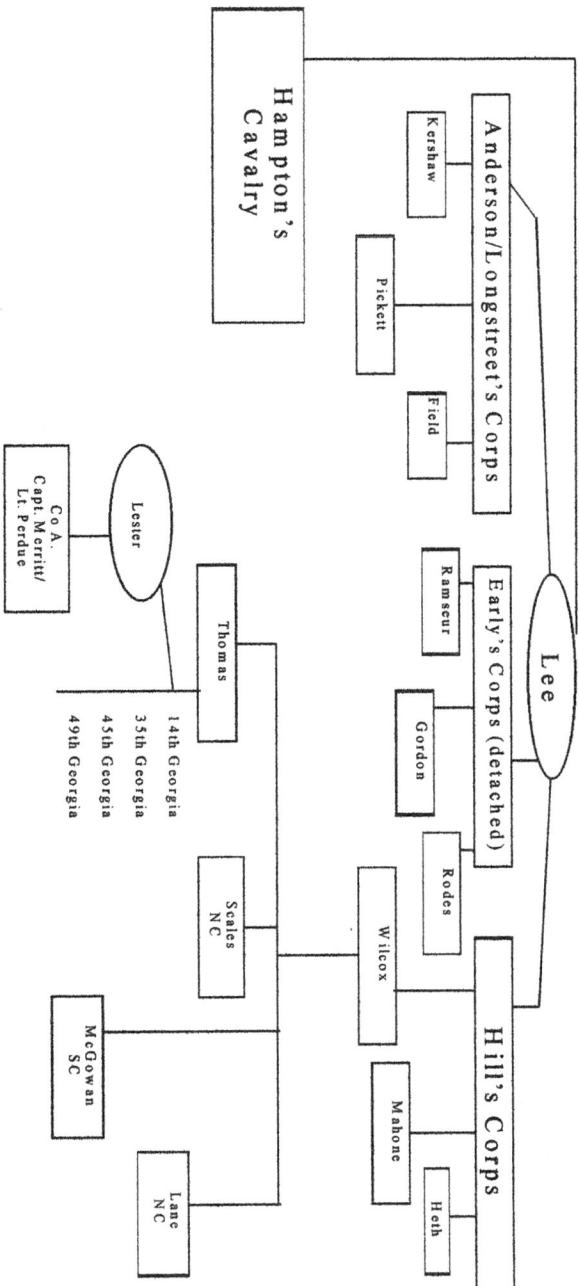

Petersburg

```
                              Lee
                               |
  ┌──────────────┬─────────────┼──────────────┐
  |              |             |              |
Hampton's   Anderson/Longstreet's   Early's Corps      Hill's Corps
Cavalry        Corps            (detached)
  |              |                  |              |
  |         ┌────┼────┐        ┌────┼────┐    ┌────┼──────┐
  |      Kershaw Pickett Field Ramseur Gordon Rodes Wilcox Mahone Heth
  |                                              |
  |                                    ┌─────────┼────────┐
Lester                              Scales    McGowan   Lane
  |                                    NC        SC       NC
Thomas
  |
14th Georgia
35th Georgia
45th Georgia
49th Georgia

Co. A.
Capt. Merritt/
Lt. Perdue
```

By mid-March, Lee's Army was depleted to about 55,000 men to face Meade's 120,000. Three of Longstreet's divisions manned the Richmond trenches. Thus Lee had just over 40,000 to man the eleven miles of Petersburg lines. Lee believed the only hope to save his army was to evacuate west to the Danville railroad junction and transport his army southward to merge with General Joseph E. Johnston in North Carolina. However, evacuation of Petersburg and the Southside Railroad meant the loss of Richmond also. Davis urged Lee instead to make one last attempt to break Meade's line. Lee complied, ordering Major General Gordon's division to lead the assault on 25 March. He attacked eastward toward City Point. Gordon did succeed in breaking the line and for a while occupied Fort Stedman in the US line, but Burnside's old corps soon closed the gap. Lee realized the attack had failed and recalled it. He lost 5,000 men. Most of those had been taken prisoner.

Meade, reasoning that Lee had to thin his lines to support this attack, attacked at several points along the line that same afternoon. Lee's lines held firm, but he lost further casualties in killed, captured, and wounded. Company A suffered no casualties, but other companies in the 14th suffered four killed and 19 wounded in this attack.

In the next few days Sheridan's cavalry began to threaten Lee's right. This possibility had worried Lee for some time, as that end of the line was thin, yet commanded important terrain guarding the railroad. Lee sent Generals Pickett and Fitzhugh Lee on a wide sweep around the end of the line at Five Forks to attack Sheridan. Pickett caused some damage to Sheridan, but failed to turn his army away. Pickett, Johnson, Lee, and Anderson entrenched at Five Forks on 1 April, leaving a gap of almost two miles in the Confederate lines from west of Burgess Mill back to Five Forks. Lee gambled that US forces would not observe this gap in the dense forest.

But Sheridan did find the gap. He requested Warren's Corps of infantry, and shortly after noon on 1 April hit Five Forks from the front, rear, and left flank. The Confederates were soundly defeated. Lee lost another 6,000 in killed, wounded, and captured. Pickett and the remaining forces fell back two or three miles to the railroad and were cut off from Lee's main force.

In eight days Lee had lost one-fifth of his army. He was left with about 30,000 troops to man the Petersburg lines. Grant instantly sensed this moment of opportunity. With Lee's lines extremely thin, he ordered a huge assault for early morning 2 April. He expected a rout and warned Sheridan to expect Lee's Army to attempt to escape west toward him, south of the Appomattox River. Lee, A. P.

Hill, Wilcox, and the entire line knew the attack was inevitable and likely unstoppable. Lee ordered a portion of Longstreet's Corps south from Richmond to help. Longstreet personally arrived in time, but his divisions were not in time to contribute much to the defense.

On the night of 1-2 April, A. P. Hill's Corps occupied six miles of the line - from Jerusalem Road to Fort Gregg, then southwest to Burgess Mill and Hatcher's Run. Wilcox' division was arranged from Ft. Gregg southwest to Burgess Mill in order of brigade Lane, Thomas, Scales, and McGowan. General Heth's division had the extreme right. The night was very dark. It was two weeks until Easter (2 April was a Sunday) and so the night's half moon set about 2 AM. Saturday had been warm, but the cool night air turned into a thin mist or fog, though most could not know that in the darkness. Lieutenant Perdue (Co. A, 14th) and all company commanders along the line must have had the men at near 100% security all night. Noise and light discipline were probably observed better tonight than at any time in the war. Lee's veterans knew what was coming, and each man could only hope his portion of the line would be spared the worst of the coming attack.

The attack commenced with a brutal artillery bombardment in the intense darkness before dawn. Every gun and mortar in the Federal line opened fire. Bruce Catton describes it on page 361 of A Stillness at Appomattox.

> "There were miles upon miles of gun positions, all the way from the Appomattox River to the works near Hatcher's Run, and from every weapon in the crescent there came the most intense and sustained volume of fire the gun crews could manage. Never before, not even at Gettysburg, had the army fired so much artillery so fast and so long. The whole sky pulsed and shuddered with great sheets of light. Jagged flames lit the horizon as the Confederate guns replied."

About one-half hour before dawn, Major General Wright's VI Corps attacked the center of A. P. Hill's line. The spearhead assault lasted less than an hour. From the US rear a surgeon watched the twinkling of Confederate musketry defend the line. As he watched, he saw "a dark gap in the center of the sparkling line, and then another gap to one side, and then a third." As he watched, the dark gaps ran together, and the line was captured. Among the thousands of casualties was General A. P. Hill, killed shortly after dawn.

Wright's assault must have hit almost squarely on Thomas' depleted brigade. It split Wilcox' division near the middle. Scales' and McGowan's brigades retreated northwest with Heth's division. Lane's brigade retreated north and east to Lee's secondary line running north to the river. Most of the 14th GA retreated east with Lane's brigade. It appears a portion of Company A retreated east with Lane and a portion retreated west with McGowan and Scales. Many who retreated east ran for the secondary line, but many sought shelter nearer at Fort Gregg.

Fort Gregg was manned by a portion of a Mississippi brigade. With the few survivors from Wilcox' division who ran there, the fort contained about 200 troops. It stood exposed a few hundred yards in front of the secondary line. We can be certain neither A.J. nor his brother James were in the fort, though many of the 14th were. This group of 200 hung on for several hours with the expectation of help from Longstreet's division. The US attacks on Ft. Gregg absorbed about 1,200 casualties before the fort was taken. Of the approximately 200 Confederate defenders, the US took 27 prisoners. The remaining 170 died fighting. The contribution these men made in slowing the US advance allowed Lee the valuable time he needed to evacuate his army from the Petersburg area.

By mid-morning, Lee realized the hopelessness of his situation and ordered an evacuation of Petersburg and Richmond in the evening darkness of 2 April. With Hill dead, Longstreet took command of that corps along with his own. Compassionately, Grant refused to attack or to shell Lee's withdrawal. Such was his confidence that the end was near.

The 14th Georgia suffered ten killed, 12 wounded, and 50 captured in the fighting of 2-3 April. All 12 of the wounded are among those captured. In Company A, Pvts James Dewberry, Arthur Rucker, and George Williams were killed. Lieutenant Baldwin Davis was wounded and captured, and Pvts William Banks, Thomas Britt, and James High were captured. It is very interesting that the casualties of Co A are evenly divided between 2 and 3 April, while the rest of the regiment lists only 2 April casualties. Aaron's brother is among those killed on 3 April.

While the casualty data are perhaps not precise enough to be dependable with respect to exact date, can we explain James' death on 3 April? The bulk of Lee's Army was engaged in no combat on 3 April. Only those units west of the breakthrough were – Generals Heth, Anderson, Fitzhugh Lee, and Pickett's divisions, plus McGowan's and Scales brigades from Wilcox' division. If we are to believe the deaths of James and two others from Co A occurred on 3 April as the roster states, we have to speculate that these men retreated west in the 2 April dawn assault and joined Scales' or McGowan's brigades. McGowan's brigade was attacked on 3 April still south of the Appomattox River just as the brigade crossed the Deep Run Creek. It appears likely that James Dewberry died in this fighting.

We do not fully develop the hypothesis of James' death. Other supporting data involve those in the 14th GA that were captured west of Petersburg on 3 April. The short eyewitness description below that, picks up at 13 October 1864, offers no help.

"October 13, 1864 a boring life laying around trenches often dodging distant sniper minnies and doing a little of that ourselves. November 28, 1864. Our own Captain John Mays, having went home with serious wounds last May as also Colonel Robert Folsom being wounded but died shortly thereafter at Richmond; on this date elections were held with John Merrit being elected as Captain. Richard Lester will be the new regimental commander. Our company, regiment, and brigade have greatly diminished in numbers and are not being replaced. And whereas we acted with emphasis on a brigade level, and still do, still its more of a regimental thing now. Regiments are pulled out and sent here and there doing different tasks and might not return for days. December 25th spent Christmas in the trenches as it was the 14th's turn and nothing over and above received as the Petersburg population was empty. Many desertions among the 1st, 7th, and 14th Tennessee regiments stationed near us. February 15th, 1865 gloom and doom. Our prospects are dimming and consternation is setting in. All of our large cities have fallen except Richmond. Our old friends among the North Carolina units are heavy with desertions. Into the trenches comes only pot stew and little of that. Homemade wooden shoes are commonplace or perhaps enemy shirts or pants tied around bare feet. March 25th 1865. Our brigade is now moved into new parts of the Petersburg line located in the southwestern portion near Hatcher's Run into trenches a couple hundred yards south of Fort Gregg. Cannon shell is coming in frequently but we are saving ourselves no doubt for the onrushers. On April 2, 1865, and near five o'clock in the morning, cannonading saturated our trenches and surrounding lines. A sea of the enemy poured over our lines and to the south of our trenches. Half veered southward, and the other half northward toward us. Our depleted numbers could never stand this assault and the bugles blew retreat. Many of our 14th regiment ran into Fort Gregg nearby which was located in between our original trenches and the strong secondary lines. The wiser ran for the secondary defense line two hundred yards behind Fort Gregg; but only a few made it. Our artillery came alive and tore great gaps into the enemy onrushers and our minnies sent them into our previously held trenches and except for the usual, the remaining portion of this day and evening was in this position. General A. P. Hill, our corps commander is dead. General Thomas is still with us. Colonel Lester was still with us. Captain Merrit, our company commander, was on furlough and our acting is Lt. Hiram Perdue with Sergeant McGinty leading Company A. After nightfall a few horses were left to shoot guns periodically and do some yelling but the rest of us started the big pullout. The artillery first, then cavalry, and lastly us foot soldiers retreated up the Boydton Plank Road into Petersburg and across the Appomattox River using the Pocahontas Bridge and northward up the River Road into freedom such as it was. We were among the last out of Petersburg shortly after midnight. The heavy rains had set in and explosions were everywhere to be heard. Rockets were firing off in different directions over the city out of control. The five bridges over the Appomattox River were blown up to fall into the rocky bottoms."

TO APPOMATTOX

With Hill killed, Longstreet took command of the III Corps, along with the portions of I Corps that were already on the Petersburg battlefield. AJ and all of Wilcox' division would finish the war under Longstreet's command. Ewell assumed command of the Richmond troops, including those remaining there of Longstreet's I Corps.

Lee ordered the evacuation of Petersburg on the night of April 2nd, with Longstreet's combined corps leading the retreat. The 14th writer claims to have crossed the Pocahontas Bridge leaving Petersburg, but more likely they used the Battersea Bridge. Lee's orders specified the Battersea Bridge for Longstreet's combined corps, and Wilcox' division would have had to pass it to get to the Pocahontas Bridge anyway. Heth's division from the former III Corps forded the Appomattox River about five miles west of Petersburg and drove northwest to join Longstreet's Corps.

Longstreet's Corps retreated out the River Road with the intention to cross to the south of the Appomattox at Bevil's Bridge. Gordon's Corps followed Longstreet. Ewell and Custis Lee headed west from Richmond to cross the Appomattox at the Genito Bridge. Anderson, Pickett, and Fitzhugh Lee remained south of the river and headed directly for Amelia, where Lee would assemble his army and then continue to Danville to join with Joseph Johnston's Army now in North Carolina.

The army struggled for two days without rations and with little sleep. Longstreet found the Bevil's Bridge uncrossable and diverted north crossing at Goodes Bridge east of Amelia. Ewell found the Genito Bridge uncrossable and planked the Mattoax railroad bridge to cross the Appomattox. Now all of the corps elements converged on Amelia on the night of 4-5 April, where rations awaited them. So Lee thought, but the Richmond train with the expected rations instead contained only munitions.

Wilcox' division arrived in the mid-afternoon of 4 April, and the men fell into camp in exhaustion and hunger. Lt. Caldwell of McGowan's brigade wrote later that the worn, hungry men of Pickett's, Johnson's, Heth's, and Wilcox' divisions looked as if they might not be able to leave camp. When Lee realized no rations waited, he set up a defensive perimeter and sent troops foraging for food. He appealed to the citizens of Amelia to feed his army. The delay cost dearly. Not until after noon of the rain-swept 5th did Lee issue marching orders.

On the evening of the 4th, Sheridan's Cavalry beat Lee to Jetersville, about ten miles east of Amelia. With Lee's delay at Amelia, Sheridan brought up two corps of infantry who entrenched on 5 April and blocked Lee's way to Danville. Longstreet's Corps led the way out of Amelia and met Sheridan's forces along the Danville tracks. Longstreet urged Lee to assault Sheridan's line as the only way to break through to Danville and to save the army. Lee could see the attack was hopeless, and diverted the whole army north to Amelia Springs and Deatonville. It was now a race to Lynchburg.

The army spent the night of 5 April near Amelia Springs. From the US lines at Jetersville, Sheridan's cavalry and Wright's infantry sped west toward Rice, while Griffin and Humphrey's divisions circled east as shown on the Appomattox retreat map. On 6 April, Lee's Army left Amelia Springs and passed through Deatonville. At the Jamestown Road between Deatonville and Riceville, Longstreet's and Gordon's Corps turned right toward High Bridge over the Appomattox, while Anderson and Ewell continued southeast toward what is today state way 307.

Leading the retreat, Longstreet escaped west, but Gordon, Ewell, Pickett, Johnson, and Anderson were engaged in three separate battlefield sites at Saylor's Creek. Sheridan and Wright hit Ewell and Anderson, attacking them along the ridge opposite the Hillman House from Little Saylors Creek. Griffin and Humphrys attacked Gordon's rear as his corps was crossing the double bridges over Saylors Creek. Gordon fought well, but lost 1,500 men. Pickett and Johnson lost their commands, and Ewell, Anderson, and Custis Lee surrendered one third of Lee's remaining army. East of Rice, Longstreet fought a successful action in which the 14th fought its last battle. Longstreet caught portions of Ord's infantry racing toward the river to cut Lee off at High Bridge. Longstreet guessed their mission and attacked with cavalry and infantry. US forces lost heavily, and Longstreet kept High Bridge open for the rest of the retreating army. The Confederates took about 1,000 prisoners.

Longstreet saved High Bridge across the Appomattox, but later failed to destroy it, and two US corps followed Lee's Army across. Lee's Army spent the night of 7 April north of Farmville. Hunger and exhaustion were beginning to take a heavy toll. Some troops received rations from the local town supplies, but Sheridan had sped west and captured the Lynchburg/Farmville supply train thus depriving Lee's Army of much needed food.

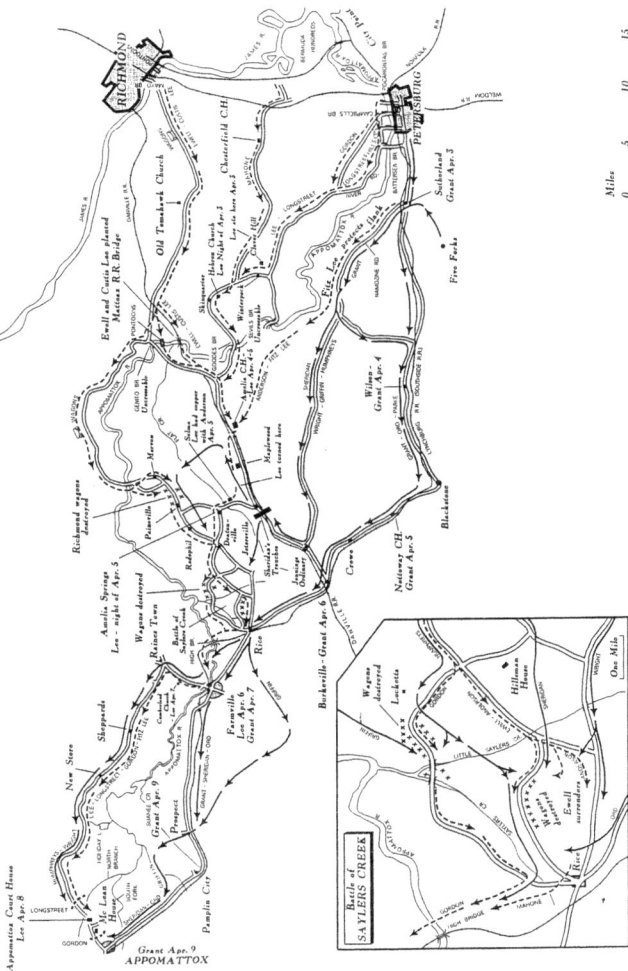

From RICHMOND and PETERSBURG to APPOMATTOX

----- Confederate Forces

——|——|—— Union Forces

Battle of SAYLERS CREEK

One Mile

Miles
0   5   10   15

111

North of Farmville the race to Lynchburg appeared lost by April 7th. Sheridan had the shortest route to the neck of land between the headwaters of the Appomattox and James Rivers. It seemed clear to both armies Lee could only fight his way to Lynchburg. For two days, the army trudged along the Raines Town-Sheppard-New Store Road toward Appomattox. Two US corps pushed the army along, while Sheridan sped north of the Appomattox River toward the village of Appomattox.

On the evening of 8 April, Lee's remaining 10,000 or so entrenched with Longstreet facing two US corps to the east and Gordon facing Sheridan's Corps to the west. Lee was cut off in both directions. The next morning, Thomas's Georgians advanced in support of John B. Gordon's troops in an attempt to open an escape route. An officer in the 14th Georgia remembered that "sharpshooters were engaged in crackling infantry fire in our front when a messenger came dashing down our lines, his horse covered with foam, crying, "Cease firing. General Lee has surrendered." Surrender came early on the Sunday afternoon of 9 April.

Thirty-six of Company A survived the morning assault of 2 April unwounded and uncaptured. They began the painful, hungry retreat west in the darkness of Sunday night. During this retreat, about three-fourths of Lee's Army evaporated. About one-third surrendered at Saylors Creek on 6 April, but the rest just gave up or deserted in foraging for food. Somehow the tough Georgians from Company A held on. Twenty-eight of the 36 who left Petersburg stuck out the weary march to surrender at Appomattox. In the regiment 12 were captured at High Bridge, Farmville, and Amelia.

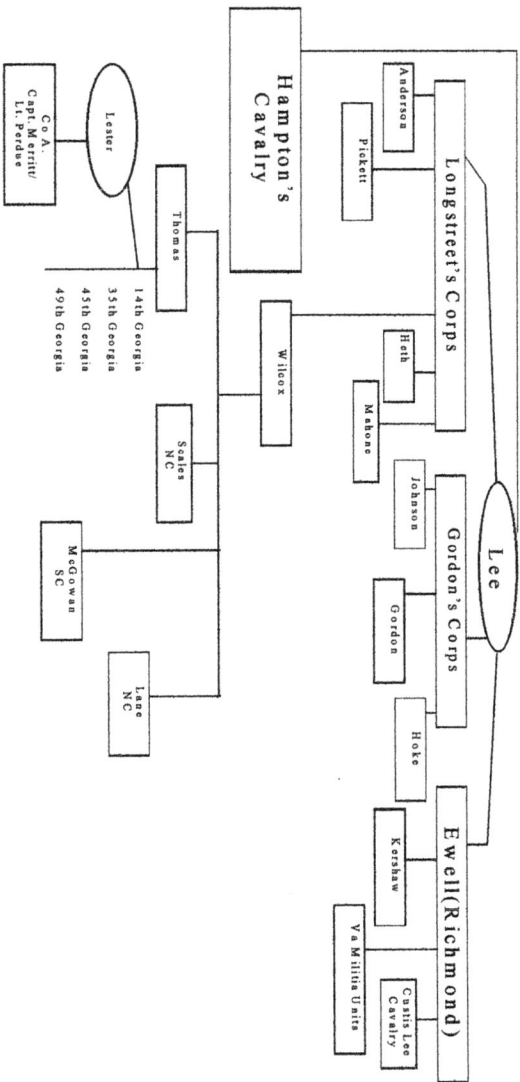

Appomattox

- **Lee**
  - **Longstreet's Corps**
    - Anderson
      - Pickett
    - Heth
      - Mahone
    - Wilcox
      - Scales NC
      - McGowan SC
      - Lane NC
    - Thomas
      - 14th Georgia
      - 35th Georgia
      - 45th Georgia
      - 49th Georgia
  - **Hampton's Cavalry**
    - Lester
      - Co A
        - Capt.Merritt/ Lt.Perdue
  - **Gordon's Corps**
    - Johnson
    - Gordon
    - Hoke
  - **Ewell(Richmond)**
    - Kershaw
      - Va Militia Units
    - Custis Lee Cavalry

The 28 soldiers from Company A of the 14th GA who surrendered with Lee at Appomattox are listed below followed by the last quotations from the Company A writer.

1st Lt. Hiram Perdue
Private Andrew H. Mays
Sergeant Major John Williams Banks
Private A. R. Mays
Private John William Bostick
First Sergeant Richard W. McGinty
Private Daniel H. Britt
Private Thomas J. Mitchell
Private Thomas Bryant
Private Phileman F. Ogletree
Corporal William C. D. Buckner
Private William J. Reaves
Corporal Charles Wesley Center
Private William M. Riddle
Private William F. Chancely
Private Enock R. Rogers
Private Tarpley L. Curtis
Private Thomas S. Sanford
Private Aaron Jackson Dewberry
Private Thomas V. Smith
Sergeant George W. Dumas
Private Alexander P. Steele
Private George W. Gilpin
Sergeant James M. Thrash
Private Matthew Tyler Gregory
Private William A. Hawthorne
Private Altonick J. Williams
Corporal John W. Williams

"On April 3rd, 1865 - following the army in the muck, mire, and cold rain, we made our way through the deep wagon ruts. There was plenty of drinking water from the rains, but no food whatever. The rain swollen creeks with overflowing banks caused our army to double back on multiple occasions. But ropes from tree to tree across the waterways was the order of the day as we wound our way to Amelia Courthouse. On April 6th, marched to a small community called Rice whereat we quickly surrounded a small enemy force of two regiments and consumed it completely to the man. The prisoners tells us they were running ahead of us to destroy bridges or to otherwise slow our line of march. We encamped north of Farmville in the evening. April 7, 1865- leaving early, we continued across a partially destroyed bridge at a narrow neck of land on the Appomattox River and onward toward the Appomattox Courthouse area. April 9th, 1865, some fighting to the west of us by General Gordon's men but by 8 AM, everything fell silent. And so it continued throughout the day as a truce held except for two shots hours apart. At the command station General Thomas ordered the final bugle blast for assembly and we were informed at 5:15 PM that our army had surrendered two hours before. A lot of Yankee wagons arrived that evening and continued into the morning of April 10th with hardtack, coffee, and loads of bread poorly cooked but greatly appreciated. April 12th morning- we marched forward to the Appomattox Courthouse and stacked our rifles and afterward divided into our own county groups and started for Danville, Virginia to hitch a rail ride homeward."

INDEX

117

REFERENCES

1. Co A 14th Georgia Letters.

2. Michener, James, Tales of the South Pacific (the MacMillan Company, NY, 1949)..

3. Randall, J. G. and Donald, David, The Civil War and Reconstruction, (D. C. Heath and Company, Lexington, MA, 1969).

4. Morrison, S. E., Commager, H. S., and Leuchtenburg, W. E., The Growth of the American Republic, (Oxford University Press, London, 1969).

5. Dowdey, Clifford, Lee's Last Campaign, (Little, Brown, and Co., Boston, 1960).

6. Davis, Burke, To Appomattox, Nine April Days, (Rhinehart & Co, New York, 1959).

7. Catton, Bruce, This Hallowed Ground, (Doubleday & Co., Garden City, NY, 1956).

8. Furgurson, Ernest, B., Chancellorsville 1863, The Souls of the Brave, (Alfred A. Knopf, New York, 1992).

9. McPherson, James, Battle Cry of Freedom, (Oxford University Press, New York, 1988).

10. Hansen, Harry, The Civil War, (Duell, Sloan, & Pearce, New York, 1962).

11. McPherson, James, Ordeal By Fire, (Alfred A.Knopf, New York, 1982).

12. Catton, Bruce, A Stillness At Appomattox (DoubleDay & Co., Inc, New York, 1954).

13. Catton, Bruce, Glory Road (DoubleDay & Co., Inc, New York, 1952).

14. Pfanz, Donald C. Staff Historian, Fredericksburg and Spotsylvania Military Park, Private Communication, April 1999.

15. Reeker, The Southern Generals.

16. Hall, George W., 14th Georgia Diary. Hargrett Library Univ. of GA.

17. Southern Historical Society Papers.

18. Private communication from Sidney Alton Dewberry, April 1993.

19. Roster of Field, Staff and Band, 14th Regiment Georgia Volunteer Infantry, E. L. Thomas' Brigade, Wilcox's Division, 3d Army Corps, Army Northern Virginia, C. S. A., private communication from Sidney Alton Dewberry, April 1993.

20. The Virginia Campaign of '64 and '65, Organization of the Army of Northern Virginia, August 184, private communication, Sidney Alton Dewberry, April 1993.

21. Antietam and Fredericksburg, Organization of the Army of Northern Virginia from August 13 to November 15, 1862, from reports of military operations during the Rebellion, Washington, Adjutant General's Printing Office, private communication, Sidney Alton Dewberry, April 1993.

22. Plato, The Golden Book of the Civil War.

ABOUT THE AUTHOR

RAY DEWBERRY is a professional writer with over fifty technical publications in the field of nuclear science and is an amateur historian with a diverse interest in U.S. history. His previous work includes an article recounting the experiences of World War II POWs that appears in a family ancestral journal. This is his first book. The research for it includes a compilation of letters from veterans of the 14th Georgia Infantry regiment, thorough use of the University of Georgia Hargrett Library and the Barnwell County Library as well as site visits to most of the Virginia campaign Civil War battlefields. The author has degrees in chemistry from Virginia Polytechnic Institute and from Florida State University. He lives with his sons in Barnwell, South Carolina.

www.ingramcontent.com/pod-product-compliance
Lightning Source LLC
Chambersburg PA
CBHW072126090426
42739CB00012B/3079